Credit for Canadians:

Everything you need to know to
fix your own credit report
and protect yourself from identity theft.

Credit for Canadians

Mike Morley

Nixon-Carre Ltd., Toronto, ON

Copyright © 2009 by Michel Morley

No part of this book may be reproduced or transmitted in any form or by any means, electronic or mechanical, including photocopying and recording, or by any information storage or retrieval system without written permission from the author, except for brief passages quoted in a review.

Library and Archives Canada Cataloguing in Publication

Morley, Michel, 1952-
   Credit for Canadians : everything you need to know to fix your own credit report and protect yourself from identity theft / Mike Morley.

Includes index.
Previous ed. published 2005 under title: The complete guide to credit and credit repair for Canadians.
ISBN 978-0-9783939-0-8

   1. Consumer credit--Canada. 2. Finance, Personal--Canada. 3. Identity theft--Canada--Prevention. I. Morley, Michel, 1952- . Complete guide to credit and credit repair for Canadians. II. Title.
HG3756.C3M67 2009   332.024'02
C2008-906596-4

Published by:
Nixon-Carre Ltd.
P.O. Box 92533
Carlton RPO
Toronto, Ontario, M5A 4N9
www.nixon-carre.com

Distributed by Ingram

Disclaimer:
This publication is designed to provide accurate and authoritative information. It is sold with the understanding that the publishers are not engaged in rendering legal, accounting or other professional advice. If legal or other expert assistance is required, the services of a competent professional should be sought. The information contained herein represents the experiences and opinions of the author, but the author is not responsible for the results of any action taken on the basis of information in this work, nor for any errors or omissions.

General Notice:
Product names used in this book are for identification purposes only and may be registered trademarks, trademarks or trade names of their respective owners. The author, Michel Morley, and the publisher, Nixon-Carre Ltd. Disclaim any and all rights in those marks.

Printed and bound in the USA

Contents

Chapter 1 - The Importance of Credit 1

Everyone needs to look at their credit report • Almost everyone experiences credit problems • A good credit rating can save you money • Who uses your credit information?

Chapter 2 - How Credit Reporting Works 11

A description of your financial transactions • Gathering credit information for your file • You can see and correct your credit report • Different rules for consumer and commercial credit •How creditors use your credit report • Protect yourself from mistakes • Automated credit decisions • The two major credit bureaus in Canada • Credit bureaus want accurate credit files • Credit files for marketing • How long items stay on your credit report • Monitoring • Fraud • Skip Tracing • Predicting delinquency • Investigative reports • Sharing your credit information • Information databases • Getting your credit report.

Chapter 3 - Understanding Your Report 25

Credit ratings and credit scores • Credit Inquiries • Refused credit • Your credit report is free • Legislation governing credit bureaus • Your rights • Contacting the Registrar.

Chapter 4 - The Banking System 41

The Canadian banking system • Returned cheques • Fraud • Kiting cheques • What to do if you have written an NSF cheque

Chapter 5 - The Sub-Prime Mortgage Crisis 51

Greed and corruption • What is a sub-prime mortgage • Fanny Mae and Freddie Mac • Why is it affecting us?

Chapter 6 - Credit Scoring 55

Credit scoring is the key to automation • FICO Scores • Credit scores are unique to each credit bureau • Credit scores can increase sales or reduce credit risk • A good credit score saves you money • Improving your credit score • The factors that affect your credit score • The importance of perceived stability • What is a "good" credit score?

Chapter 7 - Fixing Your Credit Report 67

Mistakes vs. negative information • Small mistakes can create big problems • Removing negative information • Requesting an investigation • Old items • You can't change the truth • Adding a comment to your file • Documentation is the key • Opportunities to add positive information • Unauthorized inquiries • Suing a lender • Suing the credit bureau • Submit your request in writing • Using a representative • 6 Steps to fix your own credit report.

Chapter 8 - Credit Repair Scams 83

There are no quick fixes • Laws governing credit repair firms • The past: Dumping your old credit file and starting new • Today: Your credit file stays with you • "Unique Identifiers" • Changing your name • Your Social Insurance Number • The bank loan technique • Building credit takes time • Bust Out • Falsifying employment references • Fraud and due diligence • You can do it yourself.

Chapter 9 - Understanding Your Choices 99

Pre-approved credit? • Credit agreements • Interest rates • Fixed payment or revolving credit • Grace period • Fees • Loyalty credit cards • Transferring credit card balances • Secured credit cards • The right combination of credit • Loan Application Fees • Demand loans: signature loans and lines of credit • "Calling" a demand loan • Mortgages, High Ratio vs. Conventional • Foreclosure • Mortgage insurance • First vs. second mortgage • Co-Signing • Car loans • Collateral • Lien registration • Total debt ratio vs. gross debt ratio • Not a contract under 18

Chapter 10 - Credit & Marriage 121

A rude awakening • Build your own credit • Divorce • Death • Wills • Life insurance • Power of attorney

Chapter 11 - Bankruptcy & the Alternatives 127

Who declares bankruptcy? • Bankruptcy as a last resort • Credit counselling • Meeting with a bankruptcy trustee • Trustee's fees • First meeting of creditors • Distributing the funds and winding up the bankruptcy • Secured creditors • Preferred creditors • Unsecured creditors • Discharging your debts • The final bankruptcy hearing • Family support payments & student loans • Taxes • Discharge date • Alternatives to bankruptcy • Consumer proposals

Chapter 12 - Dealing with Creditors 139

• Don't ignore your mail • Call your creditors immediately • Plan ahead for the possibility of a loss of income • Settling a debt with an unsecured creditor • Car loans • Making the harassment stop • The rules about collection calls • Consumer collections • PIPEDA privacy legislation • Personal vs. business debt

Chapter 13 - Identity Theft 153

A growing trend • What to do if it happens to you • Notifying the authorities • Tagging your credit file • Monitor new inquiries • Monitor your account statements • No one is immune • Driver's licence and vehicle ownership • Insurance fraud • Using a deceased person's ID • Birth Certificates • Protecting your documents • Fraudulent Internet sites • Personal information via email • Credit monitoring services • Ten signs that your identity may have been stolen • The Identity Theft Statement • Who are the thieves? • Losses from identity theft • Banks and credit card companies combating fraud • The credit bureaus' emergency contact info

Chapter 14 - Student Loans 179

The rising cost of tuition • Investing in your education • Student loans before August 1, 2000 • Student loans after August 1, 2000 • Credit screening • Student loans and bankruptcy • Interest • Default rate • Help from the government • The government wants its money back • Negotiating with the collection agency.

Chapter 15 - The Small Business Owner 189

Different "rules" for the self-employed • Creditors want stability • Some of your income may not be considered • Proving your income • Commercial (trade) credit for the small business owner • Small business commercial credit reports • Incorporation vs. Sole Proprietorship • Negotiating your supplier trade agreements • Collateral for small business loans • Managing your accounts receivable • Pledging your accounts receivable as collateral • Factoring your accounts receivable.

Chapter 16 - Living without credit 209

Paying cash has its advantages • Strategies for living without credit • A mortgage-free home • Mortgage interest can triple the cost of your home • Bi-weekly payments pay your mortgage faster • Cutting transportation costs • Leasing vs. Purchasing • Only use credit for assets that appreciate in value • Budgeting

Appendix A - Sample Letters 219

Sample letters that you can use to request corrections on your credit reports, or file complaints with government agencies.

Appendix B - Glossary of Credit Terms 237

Index 241

"An investment in knowledge always pays the best interest."

Benjamin Franklin

Preface

With over 25 years in the credit field, I am regularly asked by friends and colleagues for advice on how to deal with particular credit issues. They come to me because they cannot find the answers themselves. Sadly, much of the printed and Internet information currently available is not accurate and is certainly not relevant to Canadians. Because of this lack of available information, many people have unwittingly fallen prey to credit repair scams. A desire to provide a comprehensive manual on how the world of credit really works has prompted me to write this book.

Credit for Canadians is a revised and updated version of my first book, the best-selling *Credit & Credit Repair for Canadians,* and like that book, it is an insider's guide to understanding and using credit. Beginning with a look at why good credit is vital and how lenders make credit decisions, this manual explains why credit scoring is important, shows you how to avoid credit repair scams, examines the different types of credit available today, outlines the impact of bankruptcy on credit while offering alternatives, and provides common-sense strategies for guarding against the alarming increase in identity theft.

In this revised version you will also find an easy to understand explanation of the sub-prime mortgage fiasco that has caused such serious financial repercussions around the world.

Credit for Canadians answers many of the questions Canadians have about the Canadian credit reporting industry and, as the name implies, is a step-by-step guide to having the best possible credit report.

Perhaps this book should have been titled, "Everything you ever wanted to know about credit, but didn't know who to ask."

Mike Morley

The Importance of Credit

Dave (not his real name) had applied for a senior management position with a major bank's finance department. He had just been informed by the human resources department that he was the chosen candidate and that a job offer was being prepared. He was ecstatic. This was a big step up for him. Only a few small administrative details remained and the job was his.

The bank's hiring policy required that employees have perfect credit records to avoid any possible conflict of interest. The employment application included permission for credit and criminal record checks to be done. Unfortunately, when they did the credit check his credit report showed that a collection item was still outstanding. He was turned down for the job even though he was otherwise well qualified.

It turns out that a debt to a cell phone company was being reported as unpaid and had been given to a collection agency. He said that he had not paid the bill because of a dispute with the company and he thought the matter had been settled.

Eventually he managed to get this item removed from his credit report, but he never received another offer from that employer.

Everyone needs to look at their credit report

Everyone needs to know exactly what is on his or her credit report. Even if you have never been late with a payment in your life you need to know that your credit report reflects that reality. Mistakes happen every day, and mistakes on your credit report can dramatically affect your life.

The good news is that it is easy for anyone to correct errors on their credit report and avoid the headaches (and heartaches) that these errors can cause. Even if the problems being reported are true there are still some legitimate ways you can improve your credit report.

It is a fact of life. Most adults in North America suffer from a blemish or two on their credit report. These few items could be all that prevents you from getting a better job, buying your dream home, or obtaining new credit when you need it the most.

According to an article in the Toronto Sun dated November 21, 2004, business editor, Linda Leatherdale states that Canadian consumers owe an amazing $900 billion or 107% of their disposable income. U.S. consumers owe a staggering $8.4 trillion or 112% of their disposable income.

Bad credit is embarrassing, humiliating, and depressing. Many people believe that a bad credit report is indicative of a person's worth and value as a human being.

People with bad credit are not "deadbeats." Everyone wants to be able to pay their bills. People typically maintain a good credit rating until some unforeseen circumstance like a layoff, medical problem, or divorce prevents them from making a few payments in a timely manner.

Everyone struggles long and hard to pay the bills on time, but sometimes the money coming in does not quite keep up with what needs to get paid. When you're in this situation you have to carefully choose your priorities. If things get really bad, sadly enough, bankruptcy might become an attractive alternative.

If it comes down to a decision between putting food on the table and paying the credit card bill, the clear choice for most people is to look after their family first. You can be certain that even those hard-nosed, self-righteous collection agents who call and hound you to pay their bill would do the same. All their talk about how they pay their bills and expect everyone else to do the same, is just a psychological ploy intended to intimidate you. The reality is that most people are only a few pay cheques away from financial catastrophe and these telephone collectors are no different from anyone else.

By knowing, and exercising your rights, you will be well on your way to rebuilding or maintaining your credit. You will have the confidence and ability to regain your financial strength and freedom. Rebuilding a good credit record requires honesty, integrity, persistence, and vigilance from this point forward. Don't worry about the past. You cannot change it. Focus on changing your future. Improving and maintaining a good credit record will reward you and your family with a real sense of empowerment and financial freedom.

It's difficult to live without credit

It is difficult to make a purchase over the Internet without a credit card. It's not impossible, but it is certainly more convenient. The rise of companies like Ebay and Amazon has made purchasing on-line more and more common and, as a result, the use of credit cards on-line is increasing.

Very few people are able to make major purchases like homes and cars with cash. It would be great if we could, but even if you can, sometimes it actually makes more sense to preserve your cash and pay for that privilege by financing the item and paying interest over the longer term.

You cannot rent a car without a credit card. Even if you are planning on paying cash for the rental fee you still need to provide a major credit card for security. Car rental companies want to be sure that their risk of theft or damage will be covered. Hotels need your credit card for the same reasons.

Rental car companies and hotels will often get your credit card authorized for more than the value of the car rental or the hotel room in case you decide to keep the car or the room longer than you anticipated.

A good credit rating can save you money

Lenders have established interest rates for ranges of credit scores. The rate offered to you will depend on the range in which your credit score falls. For example, lower rates will be offered to clients with better credit scores. Part of the interest rate charged is to cover credit risk. Therefore, the lower the credit risk, the lower the interest rate you will be charged.

A good credit rating feels pretty good

Many people measure their sense of self-worth by their ability to possess things. And many possess these things through credit. Although they cannot pay cash in full at the time of the purchase, the option of buying on credit is available to them.

It is an unfortunate fact that, in our society, people are often judged by what they possess, such as a new car or a big home. If your credit report is good, you can choose to play this game, but if your credit report is bad you don't have that choice. There are very few creditors who will extend credit to people with poor credit histories.

Who uses your credit information?

This might surprise you.

Banks and financial services

Financial organizations such as banks, trust companies, credit unions, and investment companies, use your credit report to decide if they want you as a customer. Problems in the past with paying bills indicate a high probability of problems occurring in the future. They want to know if you have a history of bounced checks or any other type of poor financial dealing. They do not want a troublesome client. Troublesome clients are not profitable.

Lenders use your credit report to evaluate your

creditworthiness, and to determine how risky it is to extend credit to you. They decide how much to charge you for that risk based on your credit score and your credit report, whether it is for a mortgage or any other type of loan.

Credit checks by insurance companies

Insurance companies can use your credit report to help them decide if they will insure you. They want to know that you can afford the premiums over the long-term. This can also influence the price of your insurance coverage.

If you are requesting unusually large coverage, insurance companies will often look at your credit report. They will look for any excessive debts that might encourage you to make money from fraudulent claims.

Often insurance companies will do a credit check before paying a claim. If they suspect that you may have made a false claim, they will look at your credit report for any signs of living beyond your means.

Public utilities

Public utilities will insist on a credit report to find out if you have run out on any previous utility bills such as heat or electricity. They may insist on a large initial deposit, depending on what they find.

Government agencies

The government can use your credit file information without your permission to find assets that can be seized and sold to pay off a debt you owe them.

Leins

The government can also secure your assets by registering a lien against your property such as your home, your car, and the money in your bank account. A lien is defined as "a legal claim on the property of a borrower pledged as a security for the payment of a debt." This means that, if the debt is not repaid as promised, the lender (the lien holder) can enforce his/her claim and force the sale of the property to pay off the debt.

A lien does not convey ownership of the property, but gives the lien holder the right to have his or her debt satisfied out of the proceeds of the sale if the debt is not otherwise paid. Some examples include liens filed by the federal tax department (past due income tax), the family support office (child support payments), as well as provincial and municipal governments (parking fines and property taxes). These liens are a matter of public record and will show up on your credit report.

During the break in an evening seminar, one individual approached me, quite irate, about the fact that the government agency dealing with enforcing family support orders had found out where he worked and where he banked by getting his credit report without his permission. Because he was behind in his family support payments, the agency had frozen the money in his bank account and had seized part of his weekly wages.

He asked if I thought he had a case against the agency for unlawfully getting his personal credit report. I had to inform him that he had no case. The government agency had every legal right to get his credit report for the purpose of enforcing a valid court order for family support.

Government agencies and representatives are exempt from the rules restricting access to your credit report. This includes the police, the tax department, welfare agencies and family support agencies. They can request your credit report at any time to find your assets, or establish your ability to pay. Your credit report will tell them where you live, where you work, where you bank, and where you have financial dealings.

Poor credit can prevent you from getting government security clearance. If you are in a civil service job that gives you access to sensitive information, the government will perform a credit check to ascertain the likelihood of you being bribed or blackmailed because you have financial troubles.

Some professional licensing bodies may require a credit check as part of their licensing procedures.

Credit checks by the tax department

The tax department can look at your credit report if there is any suspicion that you are not reporting all of your income. Unless you pay everything with cash, your credit report will confirm your spending habits. Any evidence that points to your living beyond your means may be used to support a charge of tax evasion. You will be found guilty unless you can prove how your reported income can support your lifestyle.

Government Social Service departments can pull up your credit report to decide if you qualify for social benefits or special financial assistance.

Employment credit checks

As I pointed out in the beginning of this chapter, employers often use your credit report to help them decide if you will be hired. This is a common practice with banks and other financial services companies. Along with a criminal record check, companies hiring staff for their finance departments will often look at your credit report to determine if you are bondable. If you are in poor financial shape, it is believed, you may be tempted to be less than honest when handling the company's money.

Employers also can look at your credit report before promoting employees to higher levels of responsibility. Your promotion may involve looking after a bigger budget and approving larger expenditures. Your employer will want to know that you can manage your personal finances as well as those of the company.

Often employers will do a credit check before deciding to fire an employee. If they suspect that you may be stealing from the company, they may look at your credit report for any signs of financial difficulties, or living beyond your means.

So, as you can see, your credit report is used for far more than simply borrowing money.

"Necessity never made a good bargain."

Benjamin Franklin

How Credit Reporting Works

Your credit report describes your financial transactions. Almost every major financial transaction you are involved in gets reported to at least one of the major credit bureaus. These credit bureaus keep files on everyone. There are credit files on every small business as well.

Your credit report is a history of the accounts you have opened and how you have paid them. The companies that have extended credit to you regularly report to the credit bureau how well you are making payments. Companies where you apply for credit ask to see your credit file to see how you have paid your other accounts up to now. This is called a credit inquiry. Your credit report is made up of these inquiries and reports about how you pay your bills. When you use or make a payment on your credit card, when you pay a utility bill, or open any kind of account on credit that requires a credit inquiry, a record of that inquiry or credit payment ends up in your credit report.

Gathering information for your credit file

The information gets on your file because your creditors

report the information on a monthly basis. This reported information makes up your credit file. It is like getting a report card from your teacher at school. You are graded on your performance and a permanent record is made.

Your credit file also contains personal information such as your name, your address, your telephone number, etc. as well as public record information, including any court actions and liens against your property such as your home, car, furniture, and equipment.

Your credit report, like a school report card, lets people who have a financial relationship with you find out what "grade" you are in. The higher the grade, or credit score, the better your chance of getting a passing mark and graduating to the next level, represented by the credit limit and lower interest rate you are granted by your creditors and lenders.

You can see and correct your credit report

There is, however, an important difference between your school report card and your credit report. You never saw what was on your report card until it was given to you and your parents.

The difference is that you have the opportunity to see at any time what is on your credit report. This allows you to correct any mistakes that could come to the attention of lenders and hurt your "grade." Imagine having had the chance to see your report card before your parents saw it and having had the opportunity to improve it!

Consumer vs. Commercial credit

There is a simple, but clear distinction between consumer and commercial credit. Consumer credit is credit extended to individuals while commercial credit is credit extended to businesses, whether sole proprietorships, partnerships, or corporations.

The "rules of engagement" are different for consumer and commercial credit. While lenders cannot obtain a consumer's credit report without getting your written permission first, commercial creditors have no such restrictions and can make a credit inquiry concerning your business at any time.

How creditors use your credit report

Major creditors report everything about your financial dealings with them to the credit bureaus. They do this every month by transmitting via the Internet an electronic file. This file contains information about all their customer accounts. This information includes balance, credit limit, terms, payment information, account number, date opened, and comments.

Some government records are also transmitted every month electronically to the credit bureaus. These records include liens on property, such as a house, car, furniture and equipment, as well as all public court documents, including judgments, statements of claim, and bankruptcy proceedings.

Protect yourself from mistakes on your credit file

Unless you get a copy of your credit report and read it, you have no way of knowing what kinds of comments are on your file. An honest mistake could end up putting someone else's poor record in your credit file. It happens every day. While the credit bureaus endeavour to provide accurate information, it really is up to you to confirm the accuracy of the report. Ultimately, you are the only one who really cares about what is on your report. No one else's life is affected in the slightest when a negative comment is placed in your file, but it can change your financial and personal life dramatically.

Lenders use the Internet to access your credit report

Lenders access an individual's credit report via the Internet. Although lenders can order a credit report by telephone, the ability to instantly get a printable credit report makes the Internet the medium of choice. It allows the lender to get a credit report independently of the credit bureau's office hours and make a quick decision about whether to approve a sale.

Automated credit decisions

Today, computers make most consumer credit decisions. Because lenders have come to trust credit scoring systems, they only need to set a threshold credit score number above which their computer will automatically give an approval for the sale. The computer will decline to approve the sale if the credit score is below the threshold.

Lenders who have automated the credit approval system

never need to see the actual credit report. These lenders tend to be companies who have a high volume of transactions with a lower average dollar value per sale.

Some lenders choose to set the computer to refer the marginal scores (the ones close to the threshold) for review by their credit department. The credit department staff will look at the credit report in those few cases and adjudicate an approval or rejection.

Another situation that warrants an actual look at your credit report by credit staff will be in the case of the purchase of higher priced items such as a house, automobile or major appliance. These purchases usually involve payments over longer periods. In these cases the credit department is looking at more than just your credit score to determine your ability and willingness to pay over the longer term of the contract.

Credit bureaus are companies that are in business to make money for their shareholders. Their revenue comes from selling memberships to lenders who want to access credit reports of companies and individuals. These members pay for each report they access. The credit bureaus also earn revenue by selling trend information such as consumer buying patterns to companies who want that information for marketing purposes. For example, Ford might want to know how many cars were financed with credit last year so that they can know where they fit in the overall automobile market.

The members are buying information about consumers, like you. A critical point to understand is that the credit bureau members are the paying customers. The general public are not the credit bureaus' customers. Another way to think of it is that information about you is the inventory which credit bureaus sell to their customers, the members.

Although consumers are the source of the information that makes up the credit files, only what members report about consumers is put in the credit report. The only other sources the credit bureaus use are government public records.

The two major credit bureaus in Canada

In Canada, there are two major credit bureaus: Equifax and TransUnion. Although there are many smaller credit bureaus (approximately two thousand) that service more local or specialized markets, Equifax, and TransUnion have the lion's share of the market. Equifax and TransUnion represent at least ninety percent of all credit reports ordered by lenders in Canada. They report on both individuals and companies. Each of the smaller credit bureaus can be affiliated with Equifax and TransUnion if they wish to be.

The two reports can be quite different

Credit bureaus are companies that are in business to make money. They are in competition with each other for their customer's business. The information in your Equifax credit file is likely to be different from your TransUnion credit file. Because credit reports are expensive, many companies are members of only one credit bureau or the other. Larger companies are often members of both Equifax and TransUnion.

Different members will report different items. Therefore, the information in your two credit reports can be different. That is why you need to manage your credit reports from both Equifax and TransUnion.

When you apply for credit, a potential creditor will obtain your credit report from the credit bureau where they are a member. If the lender finds anything bad on your credit report, the lender won't check to see if you have better information elsewhere. If you are denied credit, the lender, by law, has to let you know which credit bureau report they based their decision on. But even if they say they based their decision on only one of your two credit reports you still need to look at your credit reports from both the major credit bureaus.

Credit bureaus want accurate credit files

Since this credit file information is the product that the credit bureaus sell to their members it is understandable that they want to be assured that their files are as accurate as possible. In fact, the credit bureaus have a legal obligation to ensure that the information is correct. However, they will not make a change in what a member has reported unless the member confirms the change. Understandably, credit bureaus will not take the word of the consumer without checking with the creditor first.

Ask your creditors to correct what they report

If you want to make corrections to your credit report, it is much more effective for you to convince your creditor (who is the credit bureau member) to ask the credit bureaus to make those changes for you than for you to approach the credit bureau directly.

Every new credit bureau member (creditor) needs to sign an agreement where they promise to report only what they believe to be true. The agreement also takes away any liability on the part of the credit bureau for any harm caused by a false or misleading credit report.

Since the credit bureau will modify information in your credit report only after a member (your creditor) has confirmed the new information. It is more efficient to spend your time, energy, and emotion on asking your creditors to make changes to your credit file than asking the credit bureau.

Credit files for marketing

In Canada, Equifax, and TransUnion do not sell personal information about individuals to companies that want to market consumer products and services, nor will they sell people's names to direct mail companies or information brokers and resellers. However, credit bureaus do sell information on overall buying habits. The credit bureaus will be able to give to the purchasing company valuable information about the general profile for buyers of a particular product or industry. This helps companies formulate effective marketing strategies.

Credit bureaus have other revenue streams, one of which is selling information about businesses. There is no law or statute preventing the sale of information pertaining to businesses. For a fee, the credit bureaus will prepare a pre-qualified list of businesses based on criteria specified by the credit reporting agency's business customer. These criteria can include location (by province, city, postal code), annual sales, number of employees, specific industry, the date the credit file was opened, credit score, and whether there were any negative items such as collections, returned cheques, lawsuits and judgments. According to one credit bureau web site, this information can be used to create marketing campaigns, such as telemarketing and direct mail, manage sales prospect lists, and pre-qualify potential prospects based on credit risk.

Also, "information brokers" buy business credit information from the credit bureaus to resell it to companies looking for pre-qualified clients.

Credit bureau members who report regularly

The credit bureau members who report regularly to the credit bureaus include banks, credit card companies, merchants, property management companies, and utility companies. To qualify for membership, a prospective member must show a business need for the credit reporting system, abide by the conditions of the arrangement by signing the agreement, and pay the required fee.

Some creditors do not report to the credit bureaus

Being a member of a credit bureau can be expensive so it is possible that some of your creditors might not be members of the credit bureau and so your payment history with that creditor, whether good or bad, might not show up on your report. Small landlords with only a few rental properties often do not check credit reports or report to the credit bureaus. This can be an advantage if your credit history is poor, as your late payments will not show up.

How long items stay on your credit report

How long things stay on your credit file is a matter of each credit bureau's policy. One of the determining factors includes the member's level of computer storage and sophistication. So do not assume anything. As long as a member keeps reporting an item to the credit bureau it will remain on your credit report. Get your credit reports to see if items that you had assumed to be gone are still being reported.

Paying your overdue account does not remove that record from your credit report. Just because you pay an old debt does not change or erase the fact that at one time you were not paying as you had originally agreed.

Other ways your credit report information is used

Monitoring - Fraud Databases

For a fee, the credit bureaus will provide a service for their members that watches for changes of address, new jobs, the appearance of negative items such as judgments, bankruptcies, and mortgages that are in default, and by looking at how the individual pays other lenders.

Credit bureaus can also compare the information in your credit report to information in a "fraud" database to help catch criminals.

Skip Tracing

Members can use the information in credit files to track down debtors who have run away to avoid paying their bills. Some of the clients for this service include creditors, collection agencies, lawyers who are trying to serve subpoenas, family support enforcement agencies, and the police.

Predicting delinquency

Members use the information in your credit file to predict the probability of an account becoming overdue or declaring bankruptcy.

Investigative reports

Credit bureaus prepare investigative reports for companies, primarily insurance companies and employers, who want to know more about you than what is included in your credit report. The agencies will try to find out about your character, lifestyle, reputation, etc. They will use personal interviews to collect this subjective information. This is often done before making a critical hiring decision or issuing a large insurance policy.

Unlike a credit report, credit bureaus do not have to share with you their sources of information in preparing an investigative report. Other than requiring that you give written permission for the investigative report (read the small print on the job or insurance application), there is no obligation to disclose that they have actually prepared such a report about you.

Creditors share your credit file information

Your creditors are allowed to share your credit file information with any of their affiliated companies, subsidiaries, or related businesses. For example, a large conglomerate can share your credit report information with its many divisions to sell you other products and services on credit.

Information databases

There are information databases, other than the credit bureaus, that contain personal and credit information about you. These include medical records, rent payments, cheque writing history, and insurance claims, among others. This topic, while fascinating, is beyond the scope of this book.

Getting your credit report

In Canada, getting copies of your credit reports are free by mail, but you have to pay to get your credit scores. Get the free reports if you are just checking to make sure that there are no errors, but if you will be applying for credit it is worth spending the money to get the scores. Most lenders use your credit score to approve credit. Equifax and TransUnion have independent scoring systems, so get both.

Contact information for Canadian credit bureaus:

TransUnion
P.O. Box 338, LCD 1
Hamilton, ON
L8L 7W2

If contacting them by letter you will need to include photocopies of 2 pieces if I.D.

Web site: www.tuc.ca
Email: consumer@tuc.ca
Phone: 1-800-663-9980

Equifax Canada
P.O. Box 190
Station Jean Talon
Montreal, Quebec, H2S 2Z2

If contacting them by letter you will need to include photocopies of 2 pieces if I.D.

Web site: www.equifax.ca
Email: consumer.relations@equifax.com
1-800-465-7166 to order by phone
514-355-8502 to order by fax (with 2 pieces if I.D.)

Canadian vs. U.S. credit reports

If you have ever lived in the U.S. or have dealt with U.S. based companies, you may want to check to see if you have a credit file with the U.S divisions of Equifax and TransUnion. As well, in the U.S. there is a third major credit bureau called Experian. The rules regarding getting your credit report are different in the U.S. You can get your credit report once a year for free, any more than that you have to pay for. Get your US reports online or by letter with 2 pieces of ID.

Here is the U.S. contact information:

TransUnion
Post Office Box 1000
Chester, PA 19022
Web site: www.transunion.com
Email: consumer@ transunion.com
1-877-322-8228 to order by phone

Equifax Credit Information Services, Inc
Office of Consumer Affairs
P.O. Box 740241
Atlanta, GA 30348
Web site: www.annualcreditreport.com
(accessible only from US)
1-800-685-1111 to order by phone

Experian
475 Anton Blvd. Bldg D
Costa Mesa, CA, 92626
Web site: www.experian.com
Email: customerservice@creditexpert.com
1-866-200-6020 to order by phone

Understanding Your Credit Report   3

In the past, credit reports were mysterious documents filled with strange codes that made it difficult for the average consumer to understand. But today, improvements have been made which make credit reports much easier to understand.

Credit ratings and credit scores

It is important to understand the difference between your credit score and a credit rating. A credit report will have one credit score and possibly several credit ratings.

Your credit score is a number that reflects your overall credit worthiness. It is a three-digit number between 300 and 850 with the vast majority of the population between 650 and 800. Equifax will have a credit score for you and TransUnion will have a credit score for you. These two scores are independent of each other because Equifax and TransUnion are competitors. Credit scores are not part of your credit report, they are a separate service provided by the credit bureaus that you pay extra for. More detailed information about credit scoring is covered in Chapter 4.

Credit Ratings

A credit rating is a rating such as R1 or R2 assigned to each item reported on your credit report. Since there are often many items on your credit report, and each item is "credit rated", you will have several credit ratings. The ratings are not subjective; they are assigned based on how current the balance is in the account being described.

There are several types of "credit ratings."

Here are some examples of credit ratings:

1. **PAID IN FULL AS AGREED**
    This means that your account was paid in full according to the terms of the contract. This is what you will see for a bank credit card that you pay in full very month.

2. **CREDIT LINE CLOSED BY CUSTOMER**
    This means that your account was closed at your request. An example would be your decision to close your local store account because you are moving away.

3. **TOO NEW TO RATE**
    This means that the lender feels you do not have enough payment history because your account is too new. If you just opened an account with a department store last month, there has not yet been enough time for the lender to see that you usually pay your account on time.

4. **R1 OR I1 RATING**
    This is the best rating. It means that your account is being paid according to the terms of the contract and that

there is a balance, which is not overdue.

"R1" is for revolving credit with a variable monthly payment. If it is an instalment account with a fixed monthly payment, it will be called "I1". Your bank credit card is an example of revolving credit. Your car loan is an example of an instalment account.

"R2" is not as good as "R1". "R2 or "I2" means the account is late by one payment period (usually a payment period is 30 days). "R3 or "I3" means the account is late by two periods. This continues up to "R9" or "I9".

"R9" or "I9" is the poorest rating. This means the account is at least eight periods late and that the creditor is treating your account as not collectable. For example, accounts of consumers who have declared bankruptcy will be rated "R9" or "I9" by lenders. They see little hope of ever recovering their money.

5. **DISPUTED ACCOUNT**

This means that you and your creditor are having a dispute about the balance owed. Examples of disputes are disagreements about the price, the quality of the product, the number of product units received, or a misunderstanding involving the repayment terms.

Lenders should set aside disputed items. Until they are settled, disputed items should not affect the credit approval process. Unfortunately, some lenders look at a disputed account in a negative way. They see a potentially troublesome customer. This is especially true if lenders see several disputed accounts on your credit reports.

If you regularly dispute your accounts as a way of delaying making payments because you are short of cash, creditors will pick up on your record of disputed accounts. This is the equivalent of crying "Wolf!" too many times. Your creditors will assume, as they should, that you are not willing or able to meet your payments as they become due. Creditors will be reluctant to offer you the help you need when you really do get in trouble or want to increase your credit limit.

You should not dispute your accounts as a matter of course. It should not be used as a tool to avoid paying or delaying your payments.

6. **DISPUTE AFTER RESOLUTION**
This term means that, in the opinion of the creditor, although there was an original dispute, the creditor feels, rightly or wrongly, that the dispute has been resolved.

The creditor feels that the money is owed now but you, the customer, are not satisfied with that resolution. You are still disputing the account. An example is a price reduction the lender has made that does not satisfy you. You feel it was not enough, but the lender refuses to make any more concessions.

Some prospective lenders might look at this as a sign that you are a problem customer.

7. **BANKRUPTCY**
This means that you have declared bankruptcy. Bankruptcy proceedings have not yet been wound up.

Because they have not been wound up, the debt on

this account has net yet been "erased" or "discharged" by the final bankruptcy hearing.

Bankruptcy is a matter of public record that the credit bureau will automatically pick up from government records on a monthly basis.

8. **DEBT DISCHARGED BY BANKRUPTCY**

This term means that you have declared bankruptcy and that bankruptcy proceedings have been wound up.

"Discharged" means that your debt has been "erased". At the final bankruptcy hearing, the court has recognized that you no longer have an obligation to pay the debt. Creditors can never again take action against you to collect this particular account.

9. **ACTION DISMISSED**

This means that legal action, such as a court proceeding, has been dismissed. This occurs as a result of a decision by a court judge or at the request of the creditor as a result of negotiation. Your creditor will ask the court to dismiss the case once the court is happy with the settlement.

For example, if you do not make payments as agreed, and your creditor sues you, you may not have the cash to pay. However, if you have some property of value, such as a car, you may offer the creditor the car in lieu of payment. The creditor agrees and advises the court that the action is no longer necessary. The court then "dismisses" the action and it is discontinued.

10. **DEBT UNPAID**

This means that the account is still outstanding. This rating would be used when the creditor does not know yet why the account is not paid.

11. **MAKING PAYMENTS**

This means that payments are being made on the account, but not necessarily according to the original terms.

12. **SKIP**

This means that the creditor is not able to locate the debtor. The debtor may have "skipped" town. The creditor assumes that the debtor is trying to avoid being found in order not to pay the debt.

Sometimes the debtor is not actually hiding. The debtor may have simply forgotten to advise the creditor of his new address and contact information. However, the creditor has no way of knowing this. So the creditor assumes the worst and rates the account as "skip."

Make sure you advise all your creditors of your new contact information if you move. It will avoid you being labelled as someone running away from your bills.

13. **CONSOLIDATION ORDER**

This means that the debtor is working and has considered declaring bankruptcy. The debtor has sought protection under the law from any legal action by creditors. It indicates that the creditor is hoping for at least a partial payout when the bankruptcy winds up. Compared to a conventional bankruptcy, this type of arrangement is advantageous to both the debtor and the creditors.

Under a conventional bankruptcy, the creditors would only hope to get money from any of the debtor's assets sold at "fire sale" prices to wind up the bankruptcy as quickly as possible.

Under a Consolidation Order, the debtor continues to make payments from his or her salary to the bankruptcy trustee. The trustee in turn remits to the creditors as agreed. The hope is that the wage earner can recover from these debts given enough time.

From a practical point of view, creditors have to agree in advance to take a lower amount as a settlement in return for a chance of recovering at least a part of the debt they would otherwise have lost. Otherwise, the plan has little chance of success.

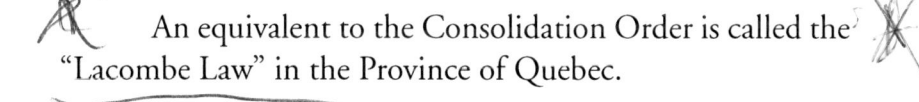

An equivalent to the Consolidation Order is called the "Lacombe Law" in the Province of Quebec.

Credit Inquiries

Every time you apply for credit, and the credit grantor checks your credit report, a credit inquiry is placed on your file. Frequent inquiries in a short time will set off an "alert" message on your credit file. However, getting your own credit report does not show up as an inquiry.

Credit inquiries can be bad for your credit score because a number of credit inquiries in a short period of time can indicate to a lender that you are a "credit seeker" and may be experiencing financial difficulties.

Too many credit inquiries

Too many credit inquiries indicate to a potential lender that perhaps your debt to income ratio is higher than you say. A potential lender that sees numerous recent credit inquiries will assume that you may have already received many of the credit lines you were asking for. The credit grantor will logically assume that the records of these debts have simply not yet shown up on your credit report. The credit grantor will think that, even if there is no evidence on your credit report, you may have current outstanding balances to these lenders and your debts may have increased. Conversely, if you do not have these other debts, the potential lender will think that these other lenders have already turned you down for some reason that he is not aware of and will naturally shy away from approving your credit request.

Fortunately, most credit inquiries drop off your credit report after two to three years.

Your signature is required

Credit reports cost lenders money. However, other than the cost, there is little to stop a prospective creditor from making a credit inquiry on you if you provide a salesperson with your personal information and agree in writing that they can get your credit report. The law requires that written consent first be obtained from every consumer credit applicant. It also requires that this written permission be obtained for each and every credit inquiry, unless the form specifically states that the applicant grants the creditor the right to make periodic credit checks.

Credit bureau members sign an agreement that stipulates that they will obtain your written permission before making an inquiry. They must keep these signatures on file for subsequent examination. This legislation lets the consumer control which lender makes a credit inquiry.

Ongoing credit checks

Creditors can make an inquiry to obtain your credit report to determine if you continue to meet their terms of credit. If you originally signed a permission form that stated that they could do a credit check "from time to time" (or language to that effect), your creditor or bank can review your eligibility to meet their credit terms at any time. This review can include a credit check. The outcome could be that your bank may decide to raise the interest rate on your credit card, or a department store could increase or decrease your credit limit on your store card.

Withdrawing your permission

It is up to you not to give that permission too easily. Beware of signing a permission form that says you are giving the lender permission to make inquiries "from time to time" or "as required." This means that the lender will be able to make inquiries as often as they feel it is necessary, verifying from time to time that you are still creditworthy. If you have already done that, you can send a letter to that lender withdrawing your blanket permission. You should monitor your credit report for any subsequent inquiries made by that creditor.

Keep in mind that if you refuse to allow ongoing credit

checks the creditor may choose to close your account.

Take action immediately if you see an inquiry made without your permission. You can report this to the lender and ask to see your signature for that particular inquiry. You should also contact the credit bureau and ask that the credit bureau follow up with the lender if you suspect that it was not simply an oversight.

It is very important that this be done in writing because you need to document your request. Documentation is essential to follow up. You will need to prove what was said and promised in case you need to escalate to Senior Management at the creditor's firm and at the credit bureau.

Reduce the number of inquiries on your credit report

Getting a copy of your own credit report does not show up as an inquiry. Always get a copy of your credit report and review it before you approach any lender. Fix any problems before you apply for credit. As much as possible, make your decision about the purchase before you start applying for credit. Do not apply at every car dealer in town trying to see who will give you the best deal.

One way you can avoid having a large number of credit inquiries showing up on your credit report when you are shopping for a mortgage is to use an independent mortgage broker who will make a single credit inquiry and shop around the banks and other financial institutions for you using that one inquiry. This will prevent multiple credit inquiries that will lower your credit score.

Refused credit

The Credit Reporting Act says: *"When you are denied a benefit or a fee has been increased, you are entitled to request, within sixty days, either the name and address of the consumer reporting agency, or the nature and source of the information that was provided."*

This means that if you have been turned down for credit or if the interest rate charged to you has been increased because of credit information in your credit report, you have a right to know which credit bureau provided your credit report along with their contact information within sixty days.

The "right" to Credit

You do not have an automatic "right" to be granted credit, even if you have a wonderful credit report. Businesses have the right to decide their terms of sale. A business or individual has a right not to do business with you. Because businesses want to make money, most will gladly sell to you on credit if you have a good record. If you refuse to provide a business a credit application, the company may decide it is not worth the trouble to sell to you at all, even for cash. It is up to both the buyer and seller to come to an agreement.

Your credit report is free

In Canada, getting your credit report costs you nothing. You can get your credit report as often as you like, within reason of course. Getting your credit score is not free. There is a fee to obtain your credit score.

Reported items

Unpaid tax and property liens can be reported as long as they remain unpaid. Credit bureaus and credit reporting agencies usually report these items only for seven years. Collections, repossessions, and foreclosures are reported also for seven years. They will remain on your credit report as long as your creditor keeps reporting the balance as outstanding in their accounts. However, most companies write off these bad debts after two or three years unless there is an arrangement for payment over time. Once the creditor stops reporting, the item will disappear in seven years.

Legislation governing consumer credit bureaus

In Canada, the provincial and territorial governments administer legislation governing consumer reporting agencies and credit bureaus. Not only do these statutes specify the kind of information consumer reporting agencies and credit bureaus can report as well as how that information can be used, they also strive to protect you against the use of outdated and inaccurate information.

The legislation recognizes that the rights of the consumer have to be balanced with the need of business to have accurate information, for example, landlords must know whether you can pay the rent and prospective employers need to know if you are bondable.

As a consumer, you should insist on ethical behaviour from businesses that collect, accumulate, amass, or make use of credit and personal information. The Credit Reporting Act says that you have a right to know what is being reported about you and to whom it is being reported. You also have a right to rectify incorrect information about yourself.

Personal information-reporting agencies

The Credit Reporting Act covers both credit-reporting agencies and personal information-reporting agencies. A credit-reporting agency keeps records of your credit transactions and information such as bankruptcies, writs, and judgements that might affect your ability to pay while a personal information-reporting agency collects information on your lifestyle and/or your credit dealings. It could include information about your character and reputation among other personal items. The agency has an obligation to attempt to verify unfavourable comments before reporting them. They cannot simply repeat gossip passed on by your neighbour.

Type of information reported

Here is what the Credit Reporting Act says about what kind of information can be reported:

"Consumer reports cannot contain a bankruptcy discharged more than seven years ago unless you have declared bankruptcy more than once. They cannot contain information about writs that represent the intention to sue, issued more than 12 months before the date of the report, unless the reporting agency has proof on file that the writ is still being pursued. Writs more than seven years old cannot be reported. They cannot contain information about the payment of taxes or fines after seven years. They cannot contain information about convictions for crimes after seven years or information about any criminal charges against you that were dropped."

You have a right to access your own credit file

The Credit Reporting Act says:

"At your request, a credit reporting agency must give you a copy of all the information contained in your credit history and personal information files. The information they give you must be easily read and in plain language."

You have the right to correct inaccurate information

The Credit Reporting Act says:

"If you find information in your file that you believe is inaccurate or incomplete, the agency must either support its claim, correct the error, make the information complete, or delete it from your file. However, you must supply proof that information is inaccurate when called upon to do so. Once the file has been corrected, the agency must notify anyone who has been given the old report within 60 days before the correction. In addition, at the request of the consumer, the agency must notify persons who received the incorrect report within the previous six months to one year, depending on the circumstances and the type of information contained in the report."

You can contact the Registrar

If you are not satisfied that your file has been updated correctly, you have the option to contact the Registrar of Consumer Reporting Agencies.

According to the Credit Reporting Act:

"When your written complaint has been forwarded to

the Registrar of Consumer Reporting Agencies, the agency will provide the registrar with the information that relates to your complaint. The registrar may inspect the files the agency has about you, and, if warranted, may order the corrections to your file. However, bear in mind that even the registrar must have your written permission before your personal file can be accessed."

The Credit Reporting Act contains some incentives to discourage the giving out of false information:

"Anyone found guilty of knowingly providing false information or contravening the Act is liable to a fine of up to $2,000 or to imprisonment up to one year, or both. A corporation committing a similar offence can be fined up to $25,000."

The Credit Reporting Act is administered by each province's Consumer Affairs Ministry. You can find the contact information for your province in your phone book under the provincial government listings.

In all my years in credit, I have personally never run across any business intentionally reporting false information.

"With money in your pocket, you are wise and you are handsome and you sing well too."

Yiddish Proverb

4

The Banking System

The Canadian Banking System

During the worldwide banking crisis of 2008 Canada was recognized internationally as having the safest and most efficient banking system in the world. Why is this?

Unlike the United States which has a fragmented banking system comprising of thousands of small, sometimes underfunded, banks, Canada has the "Big 6" Schedule 1 banks, the Royal Bank, TD, Scotiabank, CIBC, Bank of Montreal, and the National Bank which each have asset bases in the $ billions. While this limited competion among the Canadian banks can be annoying for consumers, it makes for more stringent, less flexible lending rules. There is less decision making authority at the branch level and more centralized decision making which means that a friendly branch manager is less likely to be able to approve a questionable loan for a buddy. In other words, with more checks and balances in place there is less potential for fraud.

Over the last few years new players have entered the field. We have the Schedule 2 banks, Citibank, Amex, and

ING, and the Schedule 3 foreign banks such as Bank of America and HSBC, but generally when Canadians think of banks they think of the Big 6.

Returned cheques

A returned cheque is a cheque that your bank did not honour. There are several possible reasons why your bank may not honour your cheque. The most common is that you did not have enough money in your bank account to cover the cheque you wrote. This is commonly called a NSF cheque. NSF stands for "Not Sufficient Funds." Sometimes a returned cheque will be returned "Funds Not Cleared" or "Funds Held" which means that even though you had enough money in your account the money was frozen, and not available to cover the cheque. The effect is the same. The bank has not honoured the cheque.

NSF cheques are often referred to as "bounced" cheques because when they are deposited in a bank account the money bounces out of the account again as soon as the depositing bank realizes that the cheque has not been honoured.

Creditors and returned cheques

When you knowingly write a NSF cheque, you are committing a criminal offence called fraud. Fraud implies that you intended to steal money or an item of some value from a person or company.

On the other hand, if you write a NSF cheque thinking that you had enough money in your bank account to cover the check, then, because you did not intend to defraud anyone out of any money or property, you are not committing fraud.

Fraud

There are some jurisdictions, Florida in particular, where there is a presumption of fraud when the bank does not honour a cheque. In fact, in Florida, if your cheque is returned NSF, the party to whom you made the cheque payable can call the police and ask to have you arrested. Creditors and the police in Florida take NSF cheques very seriously, something that Canadian snowbirds need to keep in mind.

I am familiar with this because of a situation I experienced when I worked as a credit manager for a Canadian firm selling to US customers. I had received a NSF cheque from a Florida customer. I called the Florida bank, on which it was drawn to ask if the funds were now available. There was no money to cover the cheque. The amount was too small to warrant hiring a local Florida lawyer to sue the customer.

Perhaps sensing my discouragement, the bank suggested that I call the local police to ask them to collect. I doubted that would help. The bank gave me the number of the police so I called to see what would happen. To my surprise, the police said yes. They took down the information and said they would "interview" the customer and call me back. I did not expect anything more to come of it.

To my astonishment, I received a call two days later saying the police had my money and wanted to know the address for sending the payment. I gave the information, thanked them, and asked what they had done to collect.

The voice on the other end chuckled and said, "Well, when we visited him at home, we told the fellow that he had a simple choice to make: he could pay us right then in cash, or we could arrest him. He said he had the money in another bank account. He volunteered to pay us out of that account. We put him in the cruiser with us and drove him to the bank. We accompanied him to the counter. He took out the money and handed it over to us. We gave him a receipt and drove him back to his house. It was as easy as flipping a pancake. We do it all the time. Nobody bounces checks in our county and gets away with it! We're pretty proud of that."

I said thanks again and hung up. I received the money three days later thanks to that Florida police department. Unfortunately, when it comes to collecting money, it is not quite that easy in Canada.

Kiting Cheques

Before the advent of computerized banking systems, desperate people could write cheques when they had no money in their account, knowing it would take a few days for the cheque to clear their bank account. They would then write another cheque from another bank account to deposit in the first one, and so on. They did this in the hope that the money to cover the cheques would arrive in time. As I already pointed out, this no longer works because of the speed with which computerized banking systems can process your cheque.

Remember, it is criminal fraud to write a cheque when you know that there are not enough funds in your chequing account.

Banks do not like NSF cheques

Your bank will probably report your NSF cheque on your credit report. Most do. If it does, your NSF cheque is there for the whole world to see.

When you open a new account, your new bank will check your credit report to verify that you do not usually bounce cheques. Banks do not want customers whose cheques have to be returned. Not only does this give the bank a poor reputation, but also it is a very expensive and time-consuming administrative process for the bank. They have to keep track of the returned cheque, document the transaction and keep records. These records have to be kept up to seven years. If you have bounced cheques in the past and the new bank sees this on your credit report, then they may choose to refuse to open an account for you on that basis.

It is astounding how many people in Canada do not have bank accounts for this very reason, and must resort to using cheque cashing/payday loan companies.

How creditors view NSF cheques

If your creditors see that you have written cheques that are not honoured by your bank, they will wonder if you have the cash to meet the commitment to make your monthly payments. They will be concerned that the cheque they get from you may also be returned.

Fees

If you write a NSF cheque to your creditor, you will be

required to not only replace the payment right away, but you may also be asked to pay an administrative fee on top of the value of the cheque.

Losing the privilege of paying by cheque

If you write an NSF cheque, you will probably lose the privilege of making future payments by cheque. Your creditor has the right to ask that you make all future payments using a credit card or some other form of secured payment such as a bank transfer or cashier's cheque or certified cheque. Your creditor may even insist on a money order.

Balance due immediately

In you bounce a cheque, your creditor may have the option to demand that you now pay the balance of the contract in full. Most credit or loan agreements stipulate that if your payments are not made on time, the balance in full becomes payable immediately.

Repossession and costs

The loan contract will probably also say that the creditor has the immediate right of repossession of any security held as collateral for the loan if you write an NSF cheque. You may be also liable for any collection costs such as legal and court costs incurred to collect the balance from you. You will also be charged the maximum allowable interest if your payments are not paid on time.

What to do if you have written a NSF cheque

Cover the cheque

What if you suddenly discover that you made a mistake and you do not have enough money to cover all the cheques you wrote? The first thing to do is to see if you can scrape together enough money (borrow from friends, dig around in the sofa cushions, cash in beer bottles, whatever) and get it deposited into your bank account fast, before any cheques are returned. That is the best-case scenario.

Tell the bank

If you cannot scrape together enough money immediately, call your bank manager or, better yet, visit the bank if possible. Ask for the manager because you need someone who has the authority to give you a temporary overdraft to cover the cheque while you arrange to cover the shortfall. Of course, you should have already established a working relationship with your bank do this, especially with the manager or senior loan officer.

Expect that you will be charged a very high rate of interest for this "favour." There will also be bank fees. However, it is much better to pay the fees and interest than suffer the consequences of a NSF cheque.

Tell your creditor

If it is too late and the cheques have already been returned, or if the bank will not approve your overdraft, the next best thing to do is to call your creditor in advance to advise that your cheque will be returned NSF by your bank. Be sure to tell your creditor that this was a mistake. Make arrangements to give your creditor a secure payment to cover the payment. Do not offer to write a replacement cheque. Your creditor will be understandably reluctant to take another cheque. Instead, offer to send a money order or to pay using your credit card.

Make the creditor feel that you are in control and that this kind of thing is a very rare event. Apologize profusely and offer to pay any fees that your creditor will incur because of the NSF cheque.

Try to get the original NSF cheque back

Once you have made the payment replacing the NSF cheque, ask the creditor to send you the original NSF cheque back to you. Otherwise, the NSF cheque could be certified as a cashier's cheque and deposited again. Also, this will keep your creditor from using the NSF cheque in any possible legal actions against you if you get in trouble financially again in the future. Document whom you talked to and be sure to get a record of your payment transaction.

If you do not receive the original NSF cheque shortly, call that same person back and follow up on that person's promise to send you back the original NSF cheque. You may not always be successful in getting the original NSF cheque back. Many companies have a policy of not returning dishonoured cheques to customers. The creditor might say that the auditors need the document. That may be true. However, if you are persistent and insist, you will probably get what you want. You have nothing to lose by trying. If the cheque is for a substantial amount and you have already replaced it, it is a good idea to pay for a stop payment to prevent it from being re-deposited. The stop payment fee is just one more expense of writing a NSF cheque.

The amount of the NSF cheque

You might not think that the amount of the NSF cheque matters, but it does. You might also think that writing a NSF cheque for five hundred dollars is worse than writing one for fifty dollars. From a creditor's point of view, the smaller the NSF cheque, the more concerned that creditor will be. If, for example, your NSF cheque is for a twenty-dollar purchase, it means that you do not have at least twenty dollars in your bank account at the time when the cheque was presented. However, if you bounce a $500 cheque because you were $20 short, at least you had $480 in your account. Twenty dollars is 100 % of a $20 NSF cheque while it represents only 4% of a $500 NSF cheque. From a creditor's point of view, getting the last twenty out of five hundred is much more likely than getting twenty dollars from someone who does not have twenty dollars in their bank account.

So don't think that because the NSF cheque is for a small amount, the creditor will not be concerned. They will be very concerned.

Avoiding returned cheques

Aside from double-checking your arithmetic in the future, another way of avoiding this kind of mistake is to set up an overdraft protection arrangement with your bank. However, you will still need to pretend you do not have it so that you will only count on it in an emergency. Using the overdraft all the time is very expensive and defeats the purpose of having it as an emergency resource. Think of it as insurance. It is good to have in place but you hope fervently that your never have to use it.

If you write several NSF cheques, you could be making yourself vulnerable to charges of fraud. The fact that you wrote several NSF cheques could be used as evidence that you had the intent to defraud. One can be a mistake, but several NSF cheques are hard to explain away as simply a series of mistakes.

The Sub-Prime Mortgage Crisis

Greed & Corruption

We've all heard the news stories about the sub-prime mortgage crisis, but the media hasn't done a very good job explaining exactly what happened.

What is a sub-prime mortgage?

Sub-prime mortgages are mortgages granted to people who have less than ideal credit, and therefore have a higher likelihood of default. Because of this higher likelihood of default they command higher interest rates to compensate for the risk. If they do not default, or if inflation pushes real estate prices upward fast enough then these sub-prime mortgages can be an attractive investment.

The sub-prime mortgage crisis started as primarily a US problem which has spread throughout the world's banks. In order to understand the crisis you need to understand how banks operate. Basically, banks borrow investors money and lend it out to other borrowers and they profit on the difference between what they pay out in interest and what they earn in interest. Often they sell bundles of these investments to other lending institutions around the world as a means of recouping their investment and spreading the risk.

It all began about 10 years ago when house prices were increasing rapidly in many parts of the US and everybody wanted in on the profits. First time homeowners were coming into the market in record numbers as well as people who had poor credit histories and previously would have had difficulty getting a mortgage. Mortgage brokers began competing to provide mortgages for these eager buyers and earn substantial commissions.

Unlike Canada, in the US the money you pay in interest on a mortgage is tax deductable, making home ownership particularly attractive. To compound the situation, up until recently, as long as you bought a more expensive property each time around, you would not have to pay any capital gains tax.

What resulted was a feeding frenzy. Everybody wanted into the real estate market. The people who qualified easily were quickly approved, but then the next batch of buyers, the "sub-prime" market who did not qualify as easily because of inadequate incomes, poor credit history, poor job prospects, or lack of down payment, wanted in on the action. As well, in an attempt to compensate for generations of social injustice the government put into place affirmative action programs intended to encourage home ownership among lower income Americans.

To cover the higher risk of default, the interest rate on the sub-prime mortgages was higher. This made the return on investment more attractive. In addition, these investments were believed to be "safe" because they were backed by real estate.

Mortgage companies wanted to earn more commissions and interest, but there was a limit to the amount of capital they had to lend out. So they decided to sell these mortgages to third party lenders at a discount to quickly get their money back so that they could earn even more commissions and interest on their capital. There was an added bonus: the risk of default was passed on to the purchaser of the mortgage. Groups of mortgages would be bundled together and sold. The credit rating agencies (different from credit bureaus) facilitated this fraud by rating the investment quality of these mortgages as being higher than they actually were.

Mortgage brokers, wanting more commissions, happily brought more business to these hungry mortgage companies. They often looked the other way when the mortgage application was not vetted properly and the due diligence in verifying the information was questionable. Nobody cared because it would not be their mortgage very long after it was approved and quickly resold.

Many of these mortgages became part of larger investment packages which the banks and financial institutions sold and resold to investors as relatively safe because the credit rating agencies rated this mortgage-backed debt as high grade. Everyone wanted in on this lucrative market and banks worldwide jumped in.

It was all based on the assumption that the original mortgage broker's documentation was accurate and that the original mortgage company had done its due diligence in verifying the information.

Unfortunately, many first-time sub-prime purchasers were approved for higher rate mortgages than they could afford to pay for very long. When they could not make the payments, they defaulted and suddenly no cash was flowing in to pay out the debt the banks were holding. In parts of the US as many as 25% of homes are in default, and financial institutions are holding mortgages that are worth far less than they paid for them.

Fannie Mae and Freddie Mac

The banks in the United States were counting on the mortgage loan guarantees from Fanny Mae and Freddie Mac (similar to our CMHC) to cover any defaults. With so many defaults house prices plummeted. The default rate was so high that both Fanny Mae and Freddie Mac announced did not have the cash to pay the banks for overdue mortgages. The U.S. government decided at the last minute to bail out both Fanny Mae and Freddie Mac temporarily by providing them with the cash to pay the bank mortgage loan guarantees. Had this bailout not occurred the result would have been unimaginable, far worse than the Great Depression of the 1930's. We still don't know if the bailout was enough.

Why is it affecting us?

The US is not suffering alone. Since banks all over the world bought these mortgages as part of their investment portfolios the pain is being felt all over the world As I write this, nobody knows how bad it will be and how long this sub-prime mortgage credit crisis will last. All we can hope is that the mortgage brokers and lenders have reined in their greed and improved their due diligence procedures.

Credit Scoring

Credit bureaus today use automated credit scoring to help with the approval of credit applications. The old method of manually reviewing and approving individual accounts was far too time consuming and labour intensive. Using modern credit scoring systems, credit bureaus are able to evaluate millions of consumer applications quickly, consistently, and impartially based on several different characteristics.

Although it may seem arbitrary or impersonal, a properly developed credit scoring system can make decisions faster and more accurately than an individual can. Equifax and TransUnion both use a credit scoring system called a "FICO score." The "FICO score" was developed by company called Fair Isaacs Company (hence the name FICO) to predict the chance of a consumer paying their bills on time.

However, some lenders will still have a credit manager make a final decision whether or not to extend credit for applications whose credit scores are close to the pass or fail mark.

Credit scores are unique to each credit bureau

Your FICO score is a number between 300 and 850. Although both credit bureaus use the same scoring algorithm (mathematical formula), your credit score may be different with each credit bureau because your information with each credit bureau might be different.

Credit scores can increase sales or reduce credit risk

Each lender decides how it will incorporate credit scores into its credit approval process. The importance it attributes to credit scores will depend on the lender's tolerance for credit risk. Lenders regularly modify the "threshold" score at which they will approve a credit application.

Here is an example of using the credit score to increase sales. Let's say that a bank has an abundance of funds that they are hoping to lend out for mortgages this month; in other words, they want to increase their mortgage business. To do this, the bank may decide to slightly lower the approval threshold, perhaps a threshold score of 760 might be decreased to accept all applicants with a score above 690 to increase sales (with an associated increase in credit risk).

Let's look at an example of using the credit score to reduce credit risk. A furniture store might decide that their level of bad debt has been too high, and it wants to reduce its credit risk exposure. So it decides to increase its threshold approval score. The higher threshold score will reduce sales by the increased amount of declined applications.

Your good credit score saves you money

Credit scoring models are used for more than just accepting or declining credit applications. Credit scores can be tools used to decide what risk is associated with ranges of scores and how much to charge for that risk. Every applicant's individual credit score will fall within a "risk" class. For example, if a particular customer scores lower than average, that customer's profile is deemed to be less ideal because the risk of not paying on time is believed to be higher than the average. The lender may have a policy that says that higher risk classes of credit applicants will be charged a higher rate of interest to reflect the higher risk associated with those classes. The lender hopes that the increase in interest revenue will more than offset the increase in bad debt write-offs that will occur in the group whose credit score is lower. So you see, if you have a higher score you can drive better deals that will save you money.

Credit scoring is based on volume

Credit scoring assumes that all customers with similar scores will behave similarly when it comes to paying their bills on time. Of course, this is not always true. However, like insurance companies, credit bureaus assume that the individual differences will disappear as the number of individuals in the group increases. In order to be effective, credit-scoring systems must be based on a large enough number of consumers to make them statistically valid.

Improving your credit score

You, the consumer, can influence your credit score by managing the factors within your control. This requires an understanding of how credit scoring works. Credit scoring involves assigning a value, usually points, to different factors that will be used to predict the likelihood of you paying your loan back as agreed.

FICO uses the following information:

- Late payments, bankruptcies, collections, and judgements (35%)
- Current debts (30%)
- How long accounts have been opened and established (15%)
- Type of credit — credit cards, bank loans, etc. (10%)
- Applications for new credit or credit inquiries (10%)

Other factors that affect your credit approval

Other than your credit score, lenders may consider additional factors to approve credit. These factors can be classified into three main categories:

1) Factors that you can influence to produce results fairly quickly, such as having a telephone in your own name, or getting a second job to increase your monthly income.

2) Factors that you can influence only in the long run, such as your age, or the number of dependents you have.

3) Factors that you cannot do anything about, such as economic conditions.

Age

Lenders assume that the older you are, the more stable your paying habits. The belief is that you have learned life's lessons in managing your money and that you will do a better job of managing your money in the future. Statistically, older individuals tend to have a higher level of income than younger people. Unfortunately, as much as we might want to, there be very little any of us can do about our age.

Marital status

If you are married, you are considered a better risk than if you are single or divorced. It may not seem relevant, but it is the stability factor at play. It is one area over which you have some influence. However, may I humbly submit that there are perhaps better reasons to get married than credit!

Number of dependents

At the risk of stating the obvious, the more dependents you have the less disposable income you have available to service your debts. You can influence this factor by deciding to have fewer children, or not having your aging parents live with you. However, these decisions are hopefully not exclusively influenced by your desire for a higher credit score.

Owner vs. Tenant

Whether you rent or own your residence will influence your credit. Although it may not seem a fair assumption, creditors believe that homeowners, as a group tend to pay their bills better than renters. It is a matter of perceived stability.

People tend to buy homes as a long-term investment. Renters lease from year to year. Renters as a group move more often.

Lenders assign the weight to this factor that they feel is appropriate, based on current economic conditions. In good times, renters tend to have a better chance of buying and often do. So they become better risks. On the other hand, in tough economic times, homeowners may suffer from a decline in property values. Lenders periodically adjust their credit decisions to reflect these changing conditions.

Credit history

The importance of credit history speaks for itself. Behavioural theory says that, given the same conditions, how you behaved in the past is a pretty good indicator of how you will behave in the future. If you have a poor payment pattern in the past, it will definitely lower your credit score.

Should you give up because you cannot change the past? Absolutely not! What you can do today is to begin managing your credit history by changing your behaviour now. How you handle your finances now will become your credit history in the future.

Credit repair firms say they can make your past disappear overnight. This is not true. However, what you can do is to begin changing your patterns right now. The benefits will take some time to show up. You must be patient.

The key is changing your habits as soon as possible and getting those positive changes reported by your creditors to the credit bureaus. Your credit history stays on your file from two to seven years, depending on the type of debt and information being reported.

Today, almost all credit card companies, banks and major lenders report payment histories electronically on an ongoing basis, usually once a month. This is the one factor over which you have the greatest influence.

Occupation

Your occupation will influence a lender's credit decision. If you are a professional such as a lawyer, doctor, or accountant, chances are that finding a job will not be such a big issue. You will tend to stay in that profession because you have spent all those years training for it.

If you work as a professional, you probably are required to belong to a professional association that demands high ethical, professional, and financial standards. Your ability to work in your chosen field will depend on keeping your membership in good standing.

If you are a skilled tradesperson you will also score higher. Skilled trades are always in high demand. However, if you are in a trade that experiences seasonal layoffs then this will reduce your score.

If you work in a growth industry, or in a larger metropolitan area, you will have a better chance of getting and keeping a higher paying job.

If you can, choose a profession or job where the likelihood of getting laid off is smaller, or the chances of finding a job with a new employer are higher. Your choice of career influences your ability to get credit.

Stability of employment

The longer you have been with the same employer, the higher your chance of getting approved. On the other hand, many people need to change employers in order to advance. These changes, although beneficial to your career, may affect the lender's credit decision. If you do change employers, but stay within the same industry, this will help moderate the negative effect.

Monthly income

If you have a higher total monthly household income, of course, you are a better credit risk. Your creditworthiness is also affected by the relationship between your monthly income and your monthly obligations. The higher the ratio of income to expenses, the higher your chance of getting approved will be.

The "type" of income can also affect your creditworthiness. Permanent employment income contributes to a better credit picture than self-employed or commission earnings.

Stability of residence

How often you move affects how your lender looks at you. By looking at your resistance to change and your corresponding stability, this factor measures the risk of you "skipping out" on your bills.

Even if you are improving your lot in life by moving up to a better, nicer, or even cheaper place to live, frequent moves may reduce your ability to get credit.

If you know that you will be moving around within a particular geographic region, one suggestion is that you get a post office box for your mail. One way that students who might be moving around frequently can help their credit is by using their parents' address as their permanent address for as long as it is feasible.

Telephone listed in your name

Some lenders will want to know if you have a residential telephone number. They may verify that you are listed in the telephone book. If you are not listed, there will be a higher risk associated with the difficulty of finding you after you have moved.

However, it is getting to be more popular to forsake the cost of a land telephone line for the convenience of a cellular telephone. Nonetheless, even if it is outdated, some lenders continue to use this factor for now. So if you can afford it, get a telephone listed in your name.

Unfairly, this can be a problem for women who often choose to have the telephone listed in the husband's name.

Economic conditions

Economic conditions will be factored into the credit decision to some extent. The employment outlook in your community and the demand for your particular skills will ultimately help or hurt you.

Economic conditions have an impact on your job situation and your ability to repay your loan. Especially if the payback period is long, as in the case of large ticket items like cars and homes, the long-term economic outlook can be an important factor to consider. There is nothing you can do to positively influence this external factor.

Monthly obligations

Credit bureau scoring systems also look at your debts and the monthly payments you make to service your debt load.

First, lenders will look at your household income to determine how well you can meet your monthly obligations. They want to confirm that you will be able to pay everything once you add in the payment for the loan for which you are applying.

Second, lenders may review the ratio of your debt load to your assets. This debt-to-asset ratio becomes more important as the repayment period of the loan gets longer. This is why you are generally asked to come up with some cash for a down payment. Mortgage lenders, for example, want to be sure that they are always owed less than the property's "fire sale" value. They want to be in a good position to recover not only the balance on your loan, but also their legal and other costs of repossession.

Financial flexibility

Lenders will also look at the flexibility in your monthly obligations. If your monthly obligations are lower, there is a better chance you can weather unforeseen situations such as a temporary job loss. An accident or sudden health problem might affect your ability to work and increase the amount of your bills. Child support payments must continue to be paid regardless of your financial situation.

You can control your monthly obligations to a great extent. Think hard before you commit to a purchase that will increase your monthly payments. You will be reducing your credit score and your financial flexibility.

Comments on your credit file

Creditors sometimes place a notice or a comment on a credit file. An example of this is when a bank puts a notice regarding fraudulent use of an ATM, such as depositing an empty envelope and then attempting to make a withdrawl. This is a very rare occurrence, but a creditor may add a negative comment to your file by mistake. Although it has nothing to do with you, the negative comment could continue to affect your ability to get credit or cost you money in higher interest.

You can not prevent errors from occurring. However, what you can do is monitor your credit report to remove errors as quickly as possible. No one else will know they are wrong except you. And you will not know unless you get a copy of your report on a regular basis.

Other factors

Additional factors can be considered by lenders. They may seem unusual. For example, some lenders keep track of the average income of your age group. A lender may believe that where you fit in that income group is related to your paying habits. The weight assigned to this kind of factor will vary from lender to lender.

The importance of perceived stability

The best thing you can do to improve your credit score is establish stability in your life. Perceived stability is a recurring theme in credit decisions. Stable people, having more to lose, it is believed, are more likely to remain at their jobs, are less likely to walk away and, therefore, more likely to continue paying on time. Stable people are easier to track down if they do stop paying.

What is a "good" credit score?

What a "good" credit score is varies from lender to lender and from time to time. It is important not to get too wrapped up in the actual number. What matters is whether the lender will approve your credit request.

The best way to find out if you have a "good" credit score is to ask various lenders what score is necessary to get approved at the present time. For example, if the bank is approving credit for people whose score is 740 and your credit score is 760, then you have a "good" credit score. If the bank moves the approval threshold from 740 to 780, then your credit score is no longer "good" enough to get approved.

Fixing Your Credit Report

It is not necessary to hire anyone to fix mistakes on your credit report. Anything that a credit repair firm can do, you can do for yourself for free. In fact, credit repair advertisements which promise to remove negative items are little more than scams.

Mistakes vs. negative information

Mistakes include things like a wrong address, a wrong date of birth, wrong spelling of your name, wrong spouse's name, wrong job, etc. These can be fixed easily by submitting documentation to the credit bureaus that proves there is a mistake on your credit report. These kinds of mistakes are relatively easy to verify and fast to fix.

Small mistakes can create big problems

I remember one couple that had applied to purchase a house. They did not end up buying the house because of mold and electrical problems that showed up during the building inspection. But a few weeks after the deal fell through the couple got a visit from the police. It turns out that the property they had been interested in buying was a marijuana "grow house"!

Apparently, a clerk at the mortgage company had put the address of the house the couple wanted to buy as the couple's current address by mistake. The credit report was then changed to reflect the change of address. Since the police can access credit reports to see who lives at a particular house, the couple were under investigation because their credit report showed the "grow house" as their current address. Of course, their driver's licenses still had their correct addresses and the police tracked them down this way. Needless to say, the couple were quite motivated to get this mistake corrected immediately!

Another example of a small mistake leading to a big problem was a case where a man, divorced for some time, had remarried. He was refused credit when he wanted to buy a house with his new bride. It seems his credit report listed his ex-wife as his current wife. His ex-wife had run up several credit cards and was not paying them. He had to pull out his divorce papers to convince the mortgage company that they were no longer married. He also sent a copy to the credit bureaus and had them separate the credit files. He also put a comment on his credit reports stating that he was not responsible for any of his ex-wife's debts since the divorce.

Removing negative information

Mistakes are relatively easy to fix, but what everyone really wants is to remove negative information. Everyone wants the negative reports from creditors changed into good ones. However, if the negative items are true, there is very little you can do to change them. Even if they are not true, contacting the credit bureaus is not the best way to get you want you want. It is usually more effective to contact the creditor who reported the error and have them correct the report.

Requesting an investigation

You have the right to dispute any information on your credit report that you feel is incorrect. The credit bureaus must re-investigate and, within a reasonable time, verify the new information.

The credit bureaus do this by contacting the particular member that originally submitted the information. The credit bureaus must then wait for an answer from that member. It may take a long time to receive a reply, especially if it is an older item. If you ask for a progress report, the credit bureaus will tell you that the matter is under investigation and that they are waiting for confirmation from the member. So you can see why it is much more effective to go to the creditor directly to get wrong information changed, rather than asking the credit bureau to do it.

Credit repair firms will often tell you that a disputed item will be erased from your credit report if the investigation is not completed in thirty days.

However, the Credit Reporting act says:

"If you find information in your file that you believe is inaccurate or incomplete, the agency must either: support its claim, correct the error, make the information complete, or delete it from your file. However, you must supply proof that the information is inaccurate when called upon to do so."

There is no stipulation with regard to a thirty-day limit. In other words, action (which may or may not include deleting the item) will be taken only after the credit bureau confirms with the member that the information is inaccurate, or can no longer be verified.

Old items

In the past, when a disputed item was more than two or three years old, many members would not respond quickly to the credit bureau's request for information because of the lack of easily accessible records. However, in today's modern computer environments, that is an increasingly rare occurrence.

In responding to the credit bureau's request, the member rarely provides the actual documentation regarding the disputed item to the credit bureau. The member may reply by letter, or only verbally, as to whether you were late, paid on time, or still have a balance.

For these older disputed items, you are better off going directly to the lender who reported incorrectly to the credit bureau in the first place. You must be persistent with the lender. It may take several attempts, but insist on getting your credit report corrected. Maybe they have changed computer systems and lost the old information, or simply will not spend the time researching the item. In that case, you might get lucky and the creditor will agree to remove the information rather than going to the trouble of verifying it.

You can't change the truth

Your credit report may contain derogatory information such as late payments and judgments. If this derogatory information is true, there is not much you can do to remove it from your credit file. The only consolation is that in time they will fall off. Most things will disappear from your credit report after seven years if everything has been settled. Bankruptcies will also come off in seven to ten years. A second one will take fourteen years to come off. A third bankruptcy may never come off.

Adding your own comment to your credit report

In an attempt to explain your situation to anyone reading your credit report, you can place a comment in your credit file. The space for your comments is about a half-page long (about three hundred words). It will allow you to tell your side of a dispute. Credit bureaus will gladly allow you to add your own comment to your credit report, unfortunately, most lenders do not read them.

Lenders do not read your personal comments because many credit decisions are automated and based solely on your credit score without looking at your credit report. As well, because most of the time consumer comments cannot be verified, the information in the comments cannot be relied upon to make a credit decision. Adding a personal comment may make you feel better, but the actual value of this statement is limited.

Documentation is the key

If you discover that one of your creditors has reported that you paid your bill late when in fact you paid on time, then send a copy of your receipt to your creditor. Request that your creditor instruct the credit bureaus to correct your file.

Unfortunately, if you do not have a receipt and you cannot otherwise prove that you paid on time, there is little you can do. You need documentation to back up what you say. Make sure you get receipts in the future.

Adding positive information

You can mitigate the effect of negative items by having as many good items as you can. Try to "crowd" the negatives off your report with as many good items as possible. Negatives items will impact your credit score less if they represent only a small portion of the items reported.

There are many ways to add positive items to your credit report. For example, having your landlord report how promptly you pay your rent is certainly positive. Unfortunately, because of the cost, most small landlords are not credit bureau members, but large property management companies usually are. Also, if you look after the payments, a secured credit card will be reported as a positive item.

Unauthorized inquiries

When you look at the "Inquiries" section, you can see which members requested your credit report. Look on the list of inquiries for anyone who was not authorized to obtain one. It may be that you simply do not remember. Call the telephone number listed for that member (every inquiry will have a contact telephone number) and ask about it. The member should be able to confirm that you applied for credit. The member should be able to provide you with a copy of the permission form you signed.

Ask the creditor to remove the unauthorized inquiry

The agreement the credit bureaus have with every member stipulates that the member undertakes to get your permission before making any credit inquiry. The credit bureaus provide your credit report to the member with that agreement in place. Therefore, the credit bureaus will only remove an inquiry from your credit report when the member requests that the inquiry be removed.

Lenders, such as department stores, banks, etc., have the power to take anything off a credit report that they put on in the first place. They might say that they cannot, but what they really mean is that it is their policy not to. Most members will agree to remove the inquiry if they cannot prove that you signed the permission form.

Suing a lender

If you believe a member obtained your credit report without your permission, in theory at least, you can sue the lender. If you win, the penalties provided by the Credit Reporting Act are substantial. In Canada, you can win upt to $25,000 in damages ($100,000 from a corporation). However, it is usually not worth the time, money, and aggravation to go to court over something like this since you must be able to prove that you experienced actual financial damages. Instead, be assertive when you point out that you did not authorize the credit inquiry and insist that the member have the credit bureau remove it.

Suing the credit bureau

Suing a credit bureau successfully is very difficult. You will have to prove the harm done by the inaccuracy in your credit report. The credit bureau only collects data supplied by its members. It relies on the membership agreement in which the member stipulates that all information supplied to the credit bureau is believed to be true.

Submit your request in writing

When you need to get in touch with the credit bureaus and lenders where you have a credit file, you should always contact them by letter. Writing creates a documentation trail. Also, by sending copies to the credit bureaus, lenders have an extra incentive for a quick resolution.

Credit bureaus and lenders ask that you submit your request by mail for two reasons. First, the credit bureaus and lenders need to verify your identity. Second, they want documentation that proves your claim. You cannot provide proof over the telephone.

When a telephone call is justified

If the item is of an urgent nature, such as an error that is affecting your ability to buy a house right now, or you have been the victim of identity theft, it makes sense to make a phone call immediately to the credit bureaus and lenders. But be sure to follow up immediately with confirming letters to document your conversations.

Be patient and persistent

Persistence and patience are what you need to get the job done. Do not stop until you get the results you want. Confirm that the corrections you were promised show up on your credit report.

Expect that your credit report will take many months to completely clean up. Replies to your requests may take several weeks. If you do not receive a reply by letter back within three to five weeks, send a follow-up letter along with all previous information. Tenacity, assertiveness, and good record keeping will yield the results you want.

Climbing the ladder

If you are having difficulty getting cooperation from a creditor, go up the corporate ladder to contact a manager or higher. Talk to the CFO if you have to.

It can be difficult to get the CFO on the phone. One trick that has worked well for me is to ask for the CFO by first name only. "Hi, this is Mike, is Dave in?" You could also say that you are returning their call. This implies that the CFO knows you. Whoever you get on the phone will be more likely to pass you on to the CFO.

The CFO's admin assistant can help you

However, to fix mistakes on your credit report you do not usually have to get the CFO on the telephone. Simply find out who the CFO's administrative assistant is. That person's job is to keep their boss free from calls like yours by dealing directly with day-to-day issues, including customers who want their credit report corrected. Be nice to this person, they have the power to fix your problem.

The CFO's administrative assistant is used to dealing with these matters. He or she will know how to get you what you want by talking to the right people. The company does not need the adverse publicity. It is far more cost effective and easier to simply fix what needs to be fixed. Be polite, but tenacious.

Using a representative

You do not need to hire anyone to improve and maintain your credit report. However, if you do not wish to do deal with the credit bureaus and lenders directly, you can have a representative of your choice deal with the credit bureaus and lenders on your behalf. You will need to provide your representative with a permission letter signed by you confirming your permission to be represented by that individual. It will alleviate any privacy protection concerns the credit bureaus might have.

Getting collection agencies to remove negatives

You can get the collection agency to agree to remove negative information on your credit report when you pay your account. If you owe an overdue balance on an account, do not be afraid to talk with the collection agency. The collection agency wants the same thing you do: to settle the account. If you are disputing the balance, and you have a good reason, explain your position and make a reasonable offer. It may take a couple of calls back and forth.

Make sure to get the collection agency's written agreement before you pay. Once the collection agency has its money, there is little incentive for them to go to the trouble of doing anything more for you.

After you have paid, confirm that the collection agency has done what it promised to do by getting a fresh copy of your credit report and verifying it for yourself. If the negative item has not been removed, contact the collection agency again to remind them that you have their written commitment to remove the negative item from your credit report.

The credit repair process

Send your request

Along with a copy of your report, send a letter to the creditor and a copy to the credit bureau. In the letter, state the facts as you see them.

Be clear about the desired outcome you want. Describe what the report says. Then explain clearly and concisely what it should be saying.

Always provide a reason for your request. You cannot be asking for a change simply to make yourself look better. You will not succeed. The report should reflect the facts, ugly as they may be. If you do not give some kind of explanation as to why you think your credit report is wrong, you run the chance of having your demand ignored. Do not try to get fancy or sound too sophisticated. Just get to the point.

Make sure that you keep copies of all correspondence and supporting documents sent to the credit bureaus and your creditors.

Send copies of documents, never send the originals.

Put a note in your calendar to follow up in case you do not get a reply. Allow about six weeks for your creditors and the credit bureaus to acknowledge receipt of your letter.

Follow up

If they agree to your request, get another copy of your credit report and confirm that the changes appear exactly as you requested.

It is more likely though, that the first time around, the change will not be exactly as you wanted or that you will not get any kind of reply or acknowledgement.

If you do not get what you want, send your letter to the next level up at your creditor's firm. Go up the food chain, get to the boss. Make sure that you include your original letter. Ask that your request be acted upon and that your letter be acknowledged along with a date by which you can expect an answer.

Never get emotional

Remember the old saying; you catch more flies with honey than with vinegar. Be polite. Do not get emotional or threatening. Human nature being what it is, if you antagonize the other person, you will not get what you want. Communicate in a business tone. If you cannot control your emotions this is where hiring someone to act on your behalf could be an advantage, because your representative will be less likely to let emotion get in the way.

Frivolous or irrelevant requests

Make sure your request is legitimate, do not cry wolf because if the credit bureaus deem your request to be "frivolous or irrelevant," they have a right not to investigate. The credit bureaus have a legal obligation to investigate all disputes that are not frivolous or irrelevant. If you convey the impression that you are a polite, but well-informed consumer that knows his or her rights, they will be glad to do what they can.

A useful technique is to compare your credit reports from the two major credit bureaus. By showing the credit bureaus and your creditors that the same item is reported differently in the two credit bureau reports, it will be obvious that one is not right and that an investigation is required to verify and correct at least one of them.

You may be asked for more information

The credit bureaus and your creditors may reply to you by asking for additional information. This is a normal. They need more information to verify your claim or to confirm your identity. They are ensuring the accuracy of the information in your credit file and protecting your identity. Help the credit bureaus and your creditors by providing as much information as possible in your first letter.

Think about all the things they might ask and provide them first. Put yourself in their shoes and ask yourself what you would need to know to make a final decision. Although you sent all the necessary documentation, you may only get a letter saying the item is under investigation. That is okay. Just make sure that you follow up.

Consistency - Documentation - Follow up

The key to successfully managing your credit report is consistency in everything you do. Follow-up is the mantra of the credit industry. You should use it too. If things do not get done as promised, and I guarantee you that most promises will be broken, you will need to act the very next day after that deadline has come and gone.

Keep a copy of everything you receive and a copy of everything you send. This serves two important purposes. First, this is will allow you to provide documentation in case you end up in court suing a creditor. Second, and more importantly, you will be learn what works well. Learning from your successful tactics and letters will improve your efficiency by saving you time, money and energy.

Make sure you note on your file copies what day you received correspondence and what day you sent out correspondence. Preferably, file all correspondence in a file for each credit bureau and each creditor.

Make sure that you set up a calendar follow-up date for the next action to be taken. That action should always be what you will do if a promise is not met or what you will do after you have verified that a promise has been kept.

The only way that you can be sure that an item on your credit report has been corrected is to confirm it by seeing it on your credit report. Get your credit report and verify with your own eyes that what you want to see is really there.

Summary -The 6 Steps to fix your own credit report

Anyone can correct their own credit report if they follow these six simple steps:

1) Get your credit report

Contact the credit bureaus by mail, telephone or the Internet. Get a free copy of your credit report from each of the two major credit bureaus. You should also get your credit score at the same time. Unfortunately, although your credit report is free, getting your credit score will cost you money. Your credit report and credit score are available over the Internet for a fee. The Internet is convenient way of monitoring your credit report and credit score in case it changes over time. For a fee, the credit bureaus also offer a service that monitors your credit report for a year and immediately sends you an alert by email if a negative item shows up.

2) Look for errors

Check both credit reports thoroughly. Look for inaccurate or missing information. If you need help understanding your report, do not be afraid to call and ask for an explanation of the codes and terms. The credit bureaus will be happy to assist you.

3) Contact the credit bureaus to correct personal information.

Contact the credit bureaus to correct your personal information such as the spelling of your name, address, employer, date of birth, spouse's name, etc.

4) Contact the member to correct financial reporting

If a credit bureau member (your creditor) has reported wrong information, such as a late payment that was not actually late, then contact the member directly. Do not contact the credit bureaus about these items. The credit bureaus only report what the member has told them. The member has an obligation to report accurately to the credit bureaus by instructing the credit bureaus to correct your credit file. The credit bureaus in turn have a duty to correct your file immediately.

5) Verify that your credit report has been corrected

Get another copy of your credit report. Make sure you see the changes that were promised to you. Follow up with your creditor and with the credit bureaus until you see those corrections.

6) Monitor your credit report

Finally, once your credit reports are free of errors or misstatements, you need to monitor them on a regular basis. Look at your credit reports at least every six months

Credit Repair Scams

There are no quick fixes where credit is concerned

Many credit repair firms promise that they can clean up your credit history virtually overnight. They say that they have quick and easy techniques for making a bad credit report look good. Regardless of what they promise, there is nothing that they can do for you that you cannot do for yourself. Also, keep in mind that if something is true you cannot get it removed just because it looks bad. If someone tells you otherwise, you would be wise to keep a firm grip on your wallet and walk away.

Laws governing credit repair firms

There are some legitimate credit consultants who provide a valuable service to the public in helping people improve their credit ratings. Unfortunately, because there are few laws governing credit repair firms, anyone can call themselves a credit consultant and set themselves up in business. Many promises are made to get consumers to fork over their hard-earned money. Unfortunately, few of those promises are kept either because the firms have gone out of business or because the promises were impossible to keep in the first place. It is up to the consumer to become better educated in matters pertaining to their credit. Making informed decisions will prevent costly mistakes.

Money back guarantee?

Some credit repair firms promise results or your money is refunded. This sounds good. Although it may seem legitimate it can be nothing more than a scam to take your money.

Exactly what results are you looking for? The word "results" is too vague. Almost everyone has something small that can be modified on their credit report. You might have a series of R9's that you want removed, but the report also has the wrong employer. If they get the employer changed but the R9's stay put is it really worth the money? They must specify in writing exactly what they will get changed for you. But even if you get a specific guarantee, by the time you realize that you are not getting any satisfying results, the company could be out of business and you would be out of luck. Sure, if you manage to track down the owner you might be able to sue them in small claims court, but keep in mind, you can't get blood out of a stone, if they have not got the money you cannot collect from them even if you do manage to get a judgment.

The past: Dumping your old file

In the past it used to be possible to "dump" your old credit file and start over new. Some "experts" still claim that it is possible to create a fresh, new credit file within

the credit bureau's computer system by erasing e
information. While this may have been possible i
certainly is not true with today's technology.

There was a time when credit bureaus filed y
report by name, using your address, your date of l... and
the name of your spouse as secondary identifiers. If you used
a slightly different version of your name, such as a slightly
different spelling or nickname, or went by an altogether
different name (for example, your married name instead of
your maiden name), the computer was not able to match the
file name to the new version. The computer by default created
a new file to store the new information. Thus, you used to be
able to create a second credit file for yourself if you knew the
system.

However, the lack of historical information in the new
file was a double-edged sword. If your previous history was
poor, it was good to "lose" it. On the other hand, not being
able to take advantage of a good previous credit history could
be a serious handicap.

Today: Your credit file stays with you

Now, the credit bureaus in Canada file all credit reports
first by social insurance number. Although many people
share similar names, addresses, employers, birthdays, and even
names of spouses, one thing that each person does not share
is his or her social insurance number. Every individual has
a unique social insurance number. This number is called a
"unique identifier". Today credit bureaus access your credit
report using your social insurance number.

Why use "Unique Identifiers"?

Credit bureaus use unique identifiers to ensure accurate identification, increase the speed of service, and accommodate the volume of requests.

Accuracy

With the advent of on-line, real-time credit systems, social insurance numbers are the only way the system can, without human intervention, positively identify your individual file. The use of a "unique identifier" is intended to prevent your private, personal information from going into someone else's file by mistake, although mistakes can still happen. However, there certainly are far fewer mistakes today than when credit files were filed by name.

Mistakes do happen

Mistakes do happen occasionally. I am familiar with one situation where a father and his family, including his adult son, immigrated to Canada. They all lived together when they first arrived.

The father and the son had the same name, including the same middle initials and the same address. Both were immigrants with landed immigrant status and, therefore, had the same first three digits in their social insurance number.

Unfortunately, the father, struggling to support his family while paying for his son's education, had a poor credit history since arriving. The son, on the other hand, landed a good job after graduating from college.

Eventually, the son tried to purchase a house. He was turned down. It turned out that the credit bureau had confused the two credit files. It took a lot of time and effort to straighten out the mix up. He has been monitoring his credit report ever since.

Volume and speed

Because so many of the purchases we make are on credit, credit systems have to be automated. Computerized credit systems use unique identifiers to handle today's ever-growing number of credit purchases.

Credit systems also have to be fast. Retail stores need to be able to process people through cash registers quickly and efficiently. The line-ups would be very long indeed if, every time you used your credit card, the store clerk had to call in for an approval, as it used to be done in the past. Automated credit systems use unique identifiers to quickly and efficiently process more and more credit transactions.

How unique identifiers work

Credit bureaus make use of your social insurance number's unique combination of numbers to trigger alarms. For example, the computer can spot false social insurance numbers.

Changing your name

Although it is legal to use an alias you must supply your true identity to obtain credit. Using an alias when entering into a contract, such as a credit purchase, is fraud.

For example, while some celebrities use aliases to protect their privacy, the obligation and the contract remain under the person's true name.

A change of name is a legal issue and a matter of public record. The credit bureaus scan these public records regularly to update all the credit files. These records include judgments, statements of claim, and changes in name, among others. You can choose to change your name if you wish, but it will not result in creating a new credit file.

If your goal is to hide the fact that you have made a name change, the computer will record the change when it cross-references your credit file from your old name to your new one using your social insurance number. This defeats the purpose of creating a new name in order to create a new credit file.

Keeping your social insurance number

Unless otherwise approved by the government, if you are changing your name, you will be keeping your social insurance number. Credit repair firms suggest that changing your name will allow you to also have another social insurance card with your new name, but with the same number printed on it. They contend that you will end up with two social insurance cards, each with the same number, but with a different name.

It does not work. Regardless of how many cards you wind up with, and how many different names you use, you will still have only one social insurance number. The credit bureau computer will always match your name and your social insurance number. The computer will make a note of the name change in your credit file that is attached to your social insurance number. There is no advantage to having two or more social insurance cards, which have the same number, but different names.

Getting a new social insurance number

To obtain a new social insurance number, you must apply to the government for permission to do so. However, unless you have a good reason to get a new social insurance number, it will not be approved. You are allowed only one social insurance number at a time.

There are special situations in which the government helps people get new social insurance numbers. Examples are persons enrolled in a witness protection program, battered wives, and anyone else whose identity needs to be changed for their protection. It is never done simply to create a new credit file.

Driver's License

I have heard of credit repair firms suggesting that you can create a new credit file by getting a new driver's license. They maintain that using your real name and a different address on your driver's license will make a "new" credit file for you. Again, this will not work because the computer system will be matching your address, driver's license number, and social insurance number. So changing your driver's license address information, or changing the driver's license number, will not fool the computer into thinking that you are indeed a different person who deserves a new credit file.

Date of birth

Even though the driver's license office might change your address on your word, they will not change your date of birth. Because you cannot change your date of birth on your ID, the computer uses your date of birth as one of the criteria for looking for your credit file. Using your social insurance number, even with a new address, will not fool the computer. It will find your file and make the appropriate changes. It will not create a new credit file. You should not pay a credit repair firm a fee for getting an address change done.

Ordering a "new" credit report

Credit repair firms suggest that if you write to the credit bureaus requesting a copy of your credit report using a new name and different personal information, the computer system will search for you and when it does not find a file for this "new" person it will create a new file.

Trying to create a new credit file by simply using a different name and address does not work because the computer will search, not only by name or by address, but will also require a combination of your social insurance number as well as your date of birth, name and address. The only way that a new file gets created is when someone is issued a new social insurance number and uses it for the first time, for example, someone applying for credit for the first time, or an immigrant first arriving in Canada and setting up a bank account.

The credit bureaus check carefully

Credit repair firms contend that the credit bureaus

cannot take the time to verify the information consumers send to them. This is not true.

Because the credit bureaus have a legal obligation to keep accurate information in their files, and because they are in business supplying information to their members, they investigate in a timely manner each and every letter that they receive from people saying that their credit file is not accurate. This is contrary to what some credit repair firms claim. They would like you to believe that it is utterly impossible for the credit bureaus to investigate even a portion of the letters that they receive, much less all of them.

Documentation and protecting your privacy

Credit bureaus prefer that you submit your requests by mail because they need documentation to verify your identity, and to confirm that the information you are providing is correct. You cannot provide documentation by telephone.

When you request your credit report by mail, the credit bureaus require that you first provide a copy of your social insurance number along with some photo ID. If you are requesting your report over the Internet or by telephone, you will be asked for your social insurance number and a credit card number. The credit card number will be used to verify your name and address. This allows the credit bureaus to cross-reference your social insurance number to access the correct credit file.

The bank loan technique

One credit repair suggestion that is floating around the internet involves the use of bank loans. This technique sounds great, but it doesn't work quite as easily as it sounds.

First you identify four banks that report to the same credit bureaus where you are building your credit file. These have to be 4 different banks, not four different branches of the same bank. You will also need to confirm that these banks have a policy of approving loans based on cash in your savings account on a dollar-for-dollar basis. You go to the first of the banks and open a regular savings account and deposit no less than one thousand dollars. After waiting for the deposit to be posted in the bank's system, you are to go back to the same bank and ask for a one-thousand-dollar loan offering your savings account as collateral. At that point, in theory, because the loan is totally secured by your savings account, the bank will give you a one-thousand-dollar loan. It will be deposited in your chequing account.

Once you have this one-thousand-dollar loan, you are to visit another bank and repeat the process. You are to go to at least three banks doing the same thing. After leaving the third bank, in theory you will still have one thousand dollars in cash in your hand. You are then instructed to go to a fourth bank and open a chequing account. You are told to use your new chequing account to make monthly payments on each of the other three bank loans.

The theory is that once you follow this plan, you will be eligible for signature loans (a signature loan means that you will sign a promissory note without any collateral), credit cards, mortgages, auto financing, or anything else you want. The premise is this: within thirty days you will have an active chequing account, three one-thousand-dollar savings accounts and three one-thousand-dollar loans on which you will be two or three months ahead on making payments. These credit repair firms say that you will also have three bank credit ratings on your credit report. And, as you continue doing this, they say you will also have a credit rating from the fourth bank.

This all sounds good but in reality finding 4 banks willing to cooperate with you will be difficult. As I explained earlier in the book, in Canada we basically have only 6 banks, unlike the United States which has thousands, so finding 4 out of the 6 that will approve something like this is unlikely. Besides, even with the loan secured by a cash deposit the bank will still want to do a credit check and will want proof of income.

Building credit takes time

If you can pull it off, this technique will begin to develop a credit history, but what you will not get is instant credit repair. Eventually, what you will get if you make the monthly payments on time over the term of the loans is a good credit rating from the three banks. It takes time and it takes discipline. What builds up your credit is not the fact that you have the loans as much as your payment record.

You must also have the cash flow to pay the interest and fees on the loans. Unfortunately, the loan interest rate will be higher given the higher risk of a relatively new customer. Although the interest earned on the savings accounts helps offset a small portion of the interest charged to you, the plan costs you money in interest and fees. Because the savings accounts were used as collateral, the bank accounts will remain frozen until the loans are paid in full.

Banks are wary of people who attempt this technique because of concern that they might be getting set-up for a type of fraud known as a "Bust Out".

"Bust Out"

A "Bust Out" is a relatively common scheme where crooks set up small credit accounts with suppliers or with banks for bank loans. They are careful to pay the accounts on time, and over a period of time the creditor gets feeling comfortable and gradually increases the credit limits. Once the limits are high enough the crooks max out the credit and then disappear.

Falsifying employment references

Some credit repair firms will tell you that you can use a false "employment reference" to qualify for larger loans than you would otherwise get.

If you have a friend who owns a business you can ask him to lie for you, or you can have a friend pretend to be an employment reference for you. The idea is that the company where you are applying for credit will call your "employer" to verify that you are working there. The lender will call for a couple of reasons. The first one is to confirm that you are a full-time employee. The second is to verify the level of income that will allow repayment of the debt. But what they do not tell you is that creditors also check to see if your bank deposits or your income tax returns confirm this information. Creditors do not only care that you are now earning this much money; they want to see a history of earnings. They want to see stability and a record of consistent earnings over time.

By getting someone to lie for you about your earnings, basically what you are telling the creditor is that you make more money than your tax return indicates. This can create all kinds of different problems for you.

Lenders verify everything

Credit repair firms will have you believe that potential credit grantors do not question an employer to verify the all the personal information you supplied. They claim that, when the creditor's staff calls, the potential credit grantors only want to know if you work there and how much money you make. That is not true. A good credit grantor will indeed verify your name, address, position, salary, and quite often, your social insurance number.

Fraud and due diligence

People can be very creative when there is money involved.

Most of the suggestions from credit repair firms constitute fraud, and it is not worth risking jail time and a criminal record to try to clean up a bad credit history. Besides, they just do not work. Most creditors will do what is called "due diligence" with every credit or loan application. They will check everything. The deal only in verified facts, or at least they should!

Besides, if you do succeed in getting the credit you are seeking, will you be able to carry the debt? If you are late with your payments you will be dramatically lowering your credit score. Also, in the event that you end up declaring bankruptcy, if the trustee investigates and finds evidence of fraud they can refuse to discharge the debt and may even recommend criminal charges.

Typing mistakes happen

In an attempt to have the least amount of human intervention possible, today's sophisticated computer systems are programmed to save time by automatically matching information that is typed into the files in the database. Nevertheless, if someone else's credit history has somehow shown up on your file when the computer tries to access your credit file, it means that someone probably typed in the wrong information.

Even with all the safeguards in place, mistakes do happen. In some rare instances, the computer may add, delete or move information based on the rules programmed into it. This is why it is so important for you to monitor your own credit report.

You can do it yourself

Credit repair firms will warn you about the huge risks in managing your own credit file. They say these risks include making things worse by "red flagging" your report and confirming negative information. This is not true. The real reason they tell you this is so you will pay them big dollars to do what you can do yourself for just the cost of postage.

After a recent educational seminar on managing your credit report, a member of the audience confided in me that she had recently been defrauded by a "credit repair" company.

She paid $2,200 in the hopes that the credit repair firm would remove negative information on her credit report. The negative information was never corrected. The only thing that disappeared was the credit repair company and her money. She lost $2,200 and still had a far less than ideal credit report.

"Life's tragedy is that we get old to soon and wise too late."

Benjamin Franklin

Understanding Your Choices 9

You will need different types of credit throughout your life. You may only require a home mortgage once, or you may buy and sell ten or more houses over the years. You may buy a number of cars. You may want to pay for your children's education. You may choose to renovate your house or go on a vacation. Whatever your financial needs are, you may decide to borrow money to meet those needs.

The range of options you will have to choose from (where to borrow the money, the interest rate, the collateral, the length of the payback period, etc.) will be greatly enhanced if you have good credit. To choose the one that best suits your life situation at the time, you will need to understand what your options are and how they work. Being familiar with the different types of credit will allow you to make better informed decisions.

Pre-approved Credit

They arrive in the mail almost daily, advertisements saying that you have been pre-approved for credit. Be wary of these ads that promise you instant credit or a major credit card regardless of your past credit record or your lack of credit history. The fact is that all legitimate creditors want to know whether you meet their criteria for credit approval. No one can guarantee you credit in advance. What these companies are doing is fishing for business. They send out thousands of these advertisements and wait to see what comes back. Read the fine print, when you sign one of these applications you are giving the company permission to do a credit check on you.

If your credit record does not meet the lender's criteria you will receive a rejection letter from the bank thanking you for applying and telling you that your request for a credit card has been denied.

Unfortunately, you still end up with an additional credit inquiry on your credit report. Remember that many inquiries in a relatively short time reduce your credit score.

What is even more disturbing is the use of these mailings as a method of stealing identities. Think carefully before you fill in and mail off one of the credit applications. Before you give them your personal information are you really sure who the recipient is? It is far safer to only apply for credit in person at your bank, or an established business.

Credit agreements

Carefully read any credit agreement before you sign it. Watch for language to the effect that you are agreeing that the lender can do credit checks at any time to monitor your account. This leaves open the possibility of multiple credit inquiries, which can lower your credit score.

Interest rate

The credit agreement should tell you how the lender calculates the balance on which interest is charged. It should also state the APR (annual percentage rate), which is the rate of interest expressed as a yearly rate.

The APR is different than the effective rate of interest. The effective rate of interest means the actual annual interest rate that includes interest on the interest. For example, if the rate is 9.65% compounded quarterly (interest is calculated and added in every third month), the effective rate is 10%. So, if you borrowed $100 at 9.65% calculated once a year, you would owe $109.65 at the end of the year. If you borrowed the same $100 at 9.65% compounded quarterly, you would owe $110.00 at the end of the year.

Another way that lenders can keep their advertised rate of interest down is by charging fees up front. If you add the fees to the interest, the amount you pay is higher. It dramatically raises the "effective" rate of interest. For example, a lender offers you a 2nd mortgage of $10,000 at 10% over 1 year. Sounds good until you add in the $2000 mortgage fee and the effective rate of interest becomes 30%. Be sure to always factor in any fees that have to be paid.

In Canada, the usury laws that prescribed the maximum loan interest rates were repealed in 1983 with the Interest Act. The Interest Act says that a lender and a borrower can agree to any amount of interest as long as it is stipulated in the contract and agreed to by all parties in writing. If there is an agreement that the borrower shall pay interest, but no rate is mentioned, the Interest Act says that the interest rate is five percent per year.

Fixed payment or revolving credit

These recommendations apply equally whether you have an instalment account (fixed monthly payment) or a revolving credit account, which requires only a minimum payment (usually five percent of the balance).

Credit Card Agreements

Grace period

A credit card agreement should spell out the grace period, which is the period of time after the statement during which you can pay off the balance before interest will be charged. You need to know what date the payment is due each month to avoid unnecessary interest.

Fees

The credit card agreement should specify what fees are applicable and how much they will be. These fees can include an annual fee, a late fee, a fee for exceeding the credit limit, NSF fees for bounced cheques, additional interest on cash advances, and an application fee.

Banks offer credit cards because credit cards are very lucrative. They make money by charging:

- Interest
- Customer user fees
- Merchant fees

Interest

One way the banks make money is by charging you, the credit cardholder, a substantial rate of interest to carry a balance past that bank's monthly "cut off" date, which is usually the 25th of the month. The banks get the money to finance your credit card from the money you deposit in your bank account, for which you receive a lower interest rate than the rate of interest charged on your bank credit card. The profitable difference in interest rates is called the "spread."

Customer user fees

Another way the banks make money is by charging credit card fees on your account. These fees can include application fees, yearly membership fees, and transaction fees. If you look at your statement and multiply the fees you pay by the number of millions of cardholders, you begin to understand why banks want you to have their credit cards.

Merchant fees

However, banks make most of their money from merchant fees. Every time you make a purchase on your credit card the bank credits the merchant's account, and assumes the risk of collecting from the consumer. For this service, the bank charges the merchant from one to six percent on each and every credit card transaction. These "merchant" fees add up to billions of dollars of revenue for the banks each year. The merchants in turn must recover the cost of the bank's fees by increasing prices to you, the consumer.

Loyalty credit cards

Lucrative merchant fees are why the banks have introduced "loyalty cards". They want you to use your credit card for day-to-day purchases such as buying groceries. Your grocer, who pays the merchant fees, in turn increases the retail price of the product in order to recover his costs. The "free" trip you thought you were getting from your loyalty credit card is paid for by you, the consumer, through higher prices and yearly "loyalty card" fees.

Increased sales through credit cards

Some credit cards are easier to get than others. Businesses understand that customers will buy more if credit is easy. Examples of these types of cards include retail store cards, and gas company cards. You are more likely to buy from merchants offering these cards than from their competition that does not offer a convenient credit card. These credit cards are a way of "capturing" their market (you). Also, they earn extra revenue for the merchant when you carry a balance and pay interest.

Transferring credit card balances

Banks will offer to pay out competing credit cards and offer you a temporarily lower interest rate because they know that most credit cardholders carry a balance. They will recover the temporary interest rate reduction many times over in the long run. Even if you do not owe a balance on another credit card, all the transaction fees from the merchants when you use their credit card will accrue to them instead of their competition.

Secured credit cards

A secured credit card is a credit card that is backed up with "security." In other words, the bank holds collateral against the credit card, usually a cash deposit.

Re-establishing credit

If you need to set up credit for the first time or if you need to re-establish your good credit record, a secured credit card can be a good tool.

Choose a reputable bank that offers secured credit cards. Choose one where your credit limit will be at least equal to the deposit required. Ask about all the fees: application fee, transaction fees, and monthly as well as yearly fees. Confirm exactly when, if ever, you will qualify to convert your secured credit card to an unsecured one.

Minimum deposit

In some cases, you must open a bank account at the same financial institution as the secured credit card. You will need a minimum deposit in that bank account. This amount varies depending on the bank you choose. The secured credit card is then issued for the amount of your deposit, which is now locked in as collateral for the secured credit card limit. You will not have access to your money on deposit with the bank and you will receive a very low rate of interest on your deposit.

An example of a secured credit card is the Home Trust Secured Visa credit card. It seems to work very well for several people that I know personally. In order to obtain the card, you must pay a security deposit when you apply along with a one-time $39.00 non-refundable account set-up fee. Your credit limit is then set at the amount of the deposit (between $1,000 and $10,000). You can increase your limit at any time by increasing the amount of your deposit. It never converts to an unsecured card. If you decide to cancel your card, you must first pay off your outstanding balance, only then will you get your security deposit back.

Read your cardholder agreement carefully. It states that you are responsible for all the fees incurred by Home Trust to collect their money from you, including legal fees. This doesn't seem fair considering they already have your security deposit, but when your credit is bad you don't have too many choices.

You will also need to consider the fees before deciding to apply for this secured card. The fees are high: a $7.50 per month service fee even if you do not use the card, a $29.00 fee when you exceed the credit limit, a $2.50 fee per ATM transaction in Canada ($4.50 for an ATM in the U.S.), and an additional 2% fee per purchase in foreign currency, including U.S. dollars. At least there is no additional annual fee.

The interest rate is just under 25% for both purchases and cash advances. Your minimum monthly payment is 3% of the balance or $10.00 (whichever is greater).

The right combination of credit

Having a credit card is a good thing since it establishes a credit record. But for the greatest impact on your credit report it is better to have different kinds of credit.

For example, if you have a bank credit card, a mortgage, and a department store credit card, this is better than having four similar bank credit cards. This will help you get higher credit limits by showing your creditors that:

- You can handle paying different types of debt.
- You budget well.

Loan Application Fees

The Loan Brokers Act says:

"No loan broker shall require or accept any payment or any security for a payment, directly or indirectly, from or on behalf of a consumer in respect of a loan of money until the consumer has actually received the loan."

In other words, you cannot be charged an application fee prior to getting your loan. The Loan Brokers Act goes further and says that:

"Before providing services or goods to a consumer to assist the consumer in obtaining a loan of money from another person, a loan broker shall provide to the consumer a clear statement in writing, showing the name, address and telephone number of the loan broker; the name of the consumer; if known, the names of the persons from whom the loan broker will attempt to obtain the loan for the consumer; the amount of the loan; the date by which the loan will be made to the consumer; and the amount that the loan broker will charge the consumer for arranging for the loan, expressed as a sum in dollars and as a percentage of the amount of the loan."

If you are being asked for a fee up front, or not being provided with a written statement outlining the above, walk away. You are not dealing with a legitimate loan broker.

Mortgage brokers are governed by individual provincial laws. In general, no mortgage broker is allowed to charge an advance fee. A legitimate mortgage broker will present you with a statement where all fees are outlined and each province sets out the time you have from the date of presentation to confirm your intentions of proceeding. The only cost you may be liable for is the appraisal fee that is paid directly to the appraiser which is payable even if you decline the mortgage.

Demand loans: signature loans and lines of credit

A demand loan can be a signature loan or a line of credit. Signature loans are loans made to you on your word alone. Your signature is sufficient to obtain the loan. Banks look carefully at your personal assets and liabilities before they will give you such a loan.

A line of credit is a loan, often secured by collateral, which can be drawn upon at any time. A signature loan is generally a fixed amount while a line of credit is a revolving account similar to a credit card.

"Calling" a demand loan

Banks can "call in" your loan (they can "demand" immediate and full payment of the balance) at any time they feel that you have become too high a credit risk. With demand loans, you usually pay the interest and service charges monthly. Your bank's exposure will always only be the original principal amount. Be sure that you go into these loans with your eyes wide open and armed with all the facts, especially regarding the risk and the cost involved if your loan is indeed "called."

Demand loans and your credit report

As long as the bank reports that you pay your demand loan well, it will help your credit report and increase your credit score. Ask the bank which credit bureau the demand loan will be reported to.

Start managing your credit report before you need it

A friend in the real estate business called me one evening and asked if I could do something to help one of her clients. She explained that her clients, a nice couple, had spent the last three months looking for a home. They had finally found the one they wanted. They both worked and could easily afford it.

They were devastated when they received a call from their bank saying they had been rejected for the mortgage financing. It had to do with a small debt of a few hundred dollars. It was a dispute over the quality of service provided by a painter three years earlier.

The painter had assigned the debt to a collection agency. The couple had told the agency that they did not feel they owed the money because of the poor workmanship. The agency said that the dispute was not their problem. So the agency went to court and obtained a default judgment.

That afternoon the bank had called to say that this judgment stood in the way of the mortgage approval. The bank's policy was to reject anyone with a judgment. As well, although the bank's mortgage took precedence over the judgment, meaning that all the money from a sale of the property would go to satisfy the bank's mortgage debt first, it was possible that the bank would not get paid in full out of the proceeds of a forced sale of the house if it was sold at too low a price by the judgment creditor.

Unfortunately, the offer on the house expired in two days. The bank refused to negotiate on this point. So the couple did not get their dream house. It could all have been prevented if the couple had been actively managing their credit report and realized that they had a judgement against them.

So, the lesson here is that you should already be monitoring your credit report, do not wait until you are ready to make a purchase. Give yourself time to fix any problems.

Mortgages

A mortgage is a legal document that pledges a property to the lender as security (a guarantee) for a payment of a debt. In other words, mortgages are loans used to buy real estate. They allow people to buy houses who would otherwise never be able to accumulate enough cash. They have been around as long as the concept of private ownership of land has existed.

Here is a little memory aid to help you differentiate between the "mortgagee" and the "mortgagor".

The mortgagor says: "I have to make my payments OR else they will take away my house."

The mortgagee says: "GEE, I have some extra money to invest, I think I'll lend it out."

Foreclosure

If all the payments are made on time, the mortgage is paid and the house is owned outright by the purchaser. Until then, if the borrower (the mortgagor) defaults on payments, the lender (the mortgagee) can "foreclose." Foreclosure means that the lender takes the house away from the borrower because the mortgage payments have fallen behind and sells it to try to get the money back.

The Great Depression of the 1930's brought about changes to the laws on foreclosure in Canada. For example, Alberta brought in the "Homestead Law" which prevented farmers from losing not only their house, but their livelihood and ability to feed their families. Under the old rules of common law, borrowers who could not make regular monthly mortgage payments would lose their property, without being able to regain title. The lender gained title and the original owner lost all rights, including any equity they had built up in their home. The National Housing Act introduced more fairness into the process. If the borrower proved the loan could be paid within a certain time frame, they would be able to redeem the property. If the repossessed house was sold by the lender for more than the balance of the mortgage, the balance (less the fees for repossessing and disposing of the property) was paid to the borrower.

High Ratio vs. Conventional

Conventional mortgages usually require at least 25% of the purchase price as a cash down payment and the remaining 75% of the purchase price is financed with a mortgage. High ratio mortgages require as little as 5% down payment, which as of February 2004 can be from gifts or borrowed funds, and the remaining 95% of the purchase price is financed with a mortgage.

Mortgage insurance

Mortgage insurance is exactly what it sounds like. It insures the lender against the borrower not making the payments. If the mortgage is in arrears, the insurer pays the mortgage lender the balance and then seizes the house to recover its money.

Because the high down payment keeps the balance of the mortgage significantly below the resale value of the house, conventional mortgages do not require mortgage insurance. High ratio mortgages, on the other hand, require mortgage insurance because the balance is close to the current market value at the time the mortgage is put in place. If you default on your payments and the mortgage company forecloses on your home, and if the sale price of the property is below the balance of the mortgage, the high ratio mortgage lender will be reimbursed the difference by the insurance company.

The two main mortgage insurance companies in Canada are The Canada Mortgage and Housing Corporation (a Crown corporation) and GE Mortgage Insurance Canada, a private sector insurance provider. As of February 2004, both

CMHC and GE have dropped the requirement for 5% cash down. They now allow you to use gifts and loans for the 5% down payment.

First vs. second mortgage

Conventional and high ratio mortgages are "first" mortgages. They are called "first" because they will be the first ones to be paid if the house is sold. A second mortgage is a mortgage borrowed after the first mortgage is in place. With the sale of a house, the second mortgage lender will get paid only after the first mortgage lender gets paid in full. Second mortgages are therefore riskier and usually demand a higher rate of interest.

Income Tax

In Canada, residential mortgage interest is not a deductible tax expense. The only time mortgage interest is deductible is when a mortgage loan is taken out to invest for a business purpose, such as investing or starting a business. Also, you do not pay tax on the profit you make (called capital gain) if you sell your principal residence. The requirement is that you live in the house while you own it.

Approving your mortgage

The bank will want to know that you have the ability and the willingness to make your mortgage payments. A mortgage is different from a bank loan:

- The mortgage is for much longer than a loan.
- The collateral for a mortgage is the real estate.

Because the mortgage is based on a long repayment schedule (usually twenty to thirty years), the bank needs to be assured of your long-term ability to pay. You have to have a good job, be a good prospect to stay employed, and earn enough money consistently over the life of the mortgage. Therefore, your stability of employment, your type of work, income level and your education are important factors in the bank's approval process.

Amount of mortgage vs. market value of the property

The value of the collateral, in this case, your home, is very important because this is a long-term commitment. The bank wants the balance owing to always remain below the market value of the house. This assures the bank that, in case you default on your payments, it can sell your house and recover the full balance owing.

Money management skills

The bank also wants to know that you are a good money manager. They will look for evidence of your financial abilities in your credit report, such as on-time payments. The bank will also want your debt-to-asset ratio to be as low as possible.

Financial flexibility

Having assets that you can call upon in times of need are a sign that you are flexible financially. You need to have the ability to find the cash to get you out of a temporary cash squeeze if you have to. This makes the bank feel comfortable that you can be trusted to manage your money in the future.

For example, if you lost your job for a month or two, the bank wants to know that you could find the money to continue making the mortgage payments.

Mortgages are usually not reported on your credit report

Most banks do not report their mortgage on your credit report because they do not want their competitors to know that you qualify for a mortgage. The bank is afraid to lose a good customer to their competitor if you were offered a better deal at another bank.

Co-Signing

When you co-sign a loan for someone else you take on the same obligation as if you borrowed that money yourself. This item will show up on your credit report as well as the borrower's credit report.

As a co-signer, although you never received the money, you owe it. If the borrowing party does not pay, the creditor will demand that you pay. If you want your money back, you will have to collect it from your "friend." Co-signing for a friend seldom works out, and is an expensive way to end a friendship. It is common for a parent to co-sign for a child who is first getting established, say for their first car loan, but after that they should be able to qualify on their own.

Settling for less with bankrupt creditors

If you owe money on your department store credit card and the store closes its doors and declares bankruptcy, your obligation to pay does not end. You still owe the money.

However, since a receiver (trustee) is being paid by the creditors to wind down the affairs of the store as quickly as possible, that receiver (trustee) will be open to negotiating a smaller payment for you to pay off your card immediately. Ask who is looking after things now that the store is closed and see what you can negotiate.

Payments to a third party

Sometimes the trustee sells the company's accounts receivable to a third party to get the money right away, less a discount, which varies from two to fifteen percent, depending on the age and size of the accounts. The third party then collects the money from customers like you. Having bought your receivable at a discount, the third party may be willing to negotiate with you a little bit. It is worth a try.

Car loans

Most automobile financing agreements permit your creditor to repossess your car at any time without advance notice and charge you for the towing and storage costs if you are late with your payments. Your creditor can keep your car even if you catch up with the payments. It may be better to sell the car yourself and pay off your debt than to incur the added costs of repossession.

Most automobile finance companies do not want to repossess your car, they just want their money. Possible exceptions are the small used car dealerships that advertise that they approve everybody regardless of their credit history. How these companies work is that they ask for a down payment equivalent to at least what they paid for the vehicle. They charge a high rate of interest and other fees (remember the discussion regarding effective rates of interest) so that if they manage to get a couple of payments out of you they are way ahead of the game. You are still on the hook for the fees. They almost hope that you will default so that they can repossess the car and resell it to someone else.

Collateral or available equity

Collateral means something of marketable value (house, mortgage, car, piece of art, etc.) that you promise to the lender in case the debt is not paid as agreed. Your favourite reclining chair may mean a lot to you, but most likely it has little market value and, therefore, has little value as collateral. Lenders do not want to repossess used furniture, and regardless of its age or condition, the minute it leaves the store it is considered used.

Strategic use of collateral

A good strategy is to give as little collateral as you can get away with. Creditors will always ask for as much collateral as possible. Strive to keep as much collateral as possible "free and clear." This strategy will leave you with additional borrowing capacity in case you have a medical or financial emergency. You can negotiate a lesser amount of collateral in most cases than what is being asked. Tying up $80,000 of equipment as collateral in exchange for a $6,000 small business loan does not make sense.

You need to keep some collateral available as leverage in negotiating with lenders. You will want to maximize the equity (market value of the item less what you owe on that item) in all your assets. Because it lowers the risk of loss to the creditor, collateral will allow you to drive down the rate of interest and possibly bargain for a better price.

Lien registration

If the item you are purchasing is used as collateral, your creditor will probably register a lien. This means that the creditor submits a document to the government in order to register the first claim against the financed item, such as a car lien. In some cases, the law will provide that a lender has a lien right, even if it is not registered. One example is auto repair shops. They can keep your car because they automatically have a lien on your car until you pay the bill. Others are plumbers, electricians, painters, etc. who automatically have lien rights against your house until you pay them.

Total debt ratio vs. gross debt ratio

Your total debt ratio reflects the relationship between your total debt and your net income after taxes. Your gross debt ratio reflects the relationship between your total debt and your income before taxes. It is a subtle difference, but make sure you understand which one is being discussed when the subject comes up.

Not a contract under 18

If you are under the age of majority (age 18 in some provinces) and enter into a contract, such as a "Music of the Month Club", the contract is not valid. A friend, whose sixteen-year old son had purchased an introductory priced

CD from a coupon in a magazine, was now receiving calls at home from a collection agency for a bill owing for unwanted items that were still arriving after more than six months. When the parents offered to return the items, they were told that their son had entered into a contract, that he owed the money, and that he was locked in for another year. When I called the collection agency's manager to explain that there was no valid contract because their son was under 18 years of age, he agreed. The company cancelled the bill, the collection agency removed the collection notice from the son's credit report and confirmed everything in writing.

If you enter into a contract before turning legal age, but reaffirm the contract afterward, it is a valid contract. For example, if you buy a stereo on credit before you are 18 and then when the collection agency calls you after you turn 18 and they ask you if you want to keep the stereo, if you say yes, you are reaffirming the contract and are liable for the balance due. If you are under 18 and your parent or guardian signed the contract as guarantor, the contract is valid, the guarantor is legally obligated to pay.

If the item is a "necessity of life" you still have to pay, regardless of your age, examples are fuel oil, and electricity. However, most of the time, young people tend to get trapped into contracts for things like music clubs, magazine subscriptions, and stereo purchases.

If you, as small business owner, are about to enter into a contract with someone under the age of majority, you need to apply to the courts to affirm the contract. Otherwise, it may not be valid. For example, a record company that wants to put a young singer under contract will ask the court for confirmation, but most of the time it is not worth the expense, it makes more sense to confirm the age of the person and then wait till they are of legal age before doing business.

The age of majority varies by province. At the time of this writing, in Alberta, Manitoba, Ontario, Prince Edward Island, Quebec and Saskatchewan, the age of majority is 18, while the age of majority is 19 in British Columbia, New Brunswick, Newfoundland and Labrador, Northwest Territories, Nova Scotia, Nunavut and the Yukon Territories.

Credit & Marriage   10

A rude awakening

The telephone, the electric bill, the lease… have always been in your partner's name. Although your credit cards have your name on them, the primary cardholder is your partner. You have been paying the bills for years but, now that you are on your own, you suddenly realize that you have no credit history.

A friend called me to ask me to help her with her credit report. Recently separated, she wanted to rent an apartment on her own. She was turned down because she had no credit history. Marrying right out of high school, everything had always been in her former husband's name up to now.

Unfortunately, there is often a "rude awakening" when people first move out on their own and they try to establish a life for themselves, or when there is a divorce or separation.

Build your own credit

The key to your credit success, regardless of your marital success, is that you build your very own credit record. If the marriage does not work out, each partner can exit with his or her own credit. Thus you don't have to be saddled with your ex-partner's poor credit history.

Establish your own accounts

If all the credit is presently in your partner's name, and you don't have a credit history of your own, have the accounts become "joint accounts." Your name, along with your partner's name, should appear on all the bills. Make sure you co-own your home if you purchase a house together. Make sure that the mortgage is in both names.

Then begin to establish accounts in your own name only. Open your own bank account. Get your own credit card. If you each drive a car, purchase one in your name only. You should be solely responsible for your own car loan. How do you do this if you haven't already got your own credit file? Over time you can leverage your joint accounts to obtain your own credit.

If you are single

If you are single now and decide to get married or to cohabitate with a partner, make sure that you keep and maintain your own credit, separate from your new partner.

In a society where many people delay marriage to establish their careers, partners with separate strong credit records are better able to maximize their family's options by taking better advantage of financial opportunities.

Divorce

In the event that the marriage ends, you will need to protect yourself by notifying all your creditors. Advise all your creditors in writing that, although you are jointly responsible for bills that exist presently, you will not be responsible for bills going forward. You should also put a note on your credit reports to this effect. Ask the credit bureaus to separate your credit file from that of your spouse. This is the especially important for women who chose to take their husband's last name.

Death of a partner

No one wants to think about it, but what would happen to your finances if your spouse passed away suddenly? Would you be able to access the family bank account to look after the arrangements? Would you be able to pay the bills while you wait for the estate to be settled? Would there be enough money to sustain you and your children until then? Would you be able to keep your creditors and the bank from taking everything you have, including your home?

Be prepared - have a joint bank account

Although for the purposes of maintaining your own credit file it is a good idea for you have separate credit files and bank accounts, it is also a good idea to set things up so that you both have access to money when you need it most. Your main checking account should be in both names. In

Canada, the money in the joint account will not be frozen after your spouse passes away. This provision is included in the application to open a joint account at banks in Canada. However, if the account is in the deceased's name only, the funds will be frozen. You will not have access to this money until the estate is settled or released by the trustee. In complicated cases it can take years to settle the estate and access the funds.

Wills

There is an old saying: "A person who dies without a will has lawyers for beneficiaries." Everyone needs to have a will, even if you do not think you have any assets. Who knows, maybe you will be hit by a bus and there will be a huge insurance payout to your beneficiaries.

No will means the government decides

Your particular situation may not be covered by the general government rules. A will prevents the government from seizing your assets and ensures that your assets are distributed the way you would want them to be.

Distribution of your assets according to your wishes

The government guidelines for the distribution of assets work fine in most cases, but what if your situation is different? For example, what if your adult kids are ungrateful brats who have not had anything to do with you for years and your sister-in-law has been your best friend throughout your life and has nursed you through your last months? Even though you have expressed verbally your wish to leave everything to your sister-in-law, without a will, the estate would go to your children (and their lawyers), leaving nothing for your sister-in-law. Better to make a will and be sure of how your estate will be distributed.

Life insurance

In your life insurance policies, you should designate your spouse or children as beneficiaries as opposed to naming your estate. The insurance money will usually pay out to the beneficiary relatively quickly giving them money to live on while the estate is still being settled. If you name your estate as beneficiary of your insurance policy, your creditors can sue your estate and take assets that you had intended to leave to your spouse and children.

Power of attorney

Spouses should grant each other power of attorney. If one spouse becomes mentally incompetent or physically disabled, the other will be able to make decisions concerning their care and assets. To make a valid power of attorney, you must be 18 years of age or more and mentally capable. You can name more than one person as your attorney if you desire.

In this case, the word attorney does not mean lawyer, it just means legal representative. You can have your lawyer draw up the power of attorney forms when you are getting your wills done, however, you can also do it yourself by picking up power of attorney forms at banks, hospitals or on the internet. The law requires that two people witness your signature. Both of the witnesses must be present together when you sign. It is not necessary to register the power of attorney for property anywhere for it to be valid.

You have the right to cancel the power of attorney at any time, as long as you are capable, by writing the revocation down on paper, signing and dating it, and having it witnessed in the same way as the original document. If you cancel your power of attorney be sure to notify the person(s) to whom you originally granted the power of attorney, financial institutions, and all the people you originally notified regarding your power of attorney.

Bankruptcy & The Alternatives   11

Who declares bankruptcy?

There is a misconception that people who resort to bankruptcy are low-income earners or people who have lost their source of income, either because they have lost their job or because their business has failed. This is not true.

High wage earners fit the profile better and are more often involved in a personal bankruptcy than lower income earners. If you think about it, it is easier to get more credit and get in debt in the first place if you earn more. The more you earn, the greater your capacity for debt. Unfortunately, if your debt level is high in relation to your income, you are vulnerable to a sudden drop in income. It is almost impossible to reduce your debt as quickly as your income has dropped.

Bankruptcy should be your last resort because:

- It can be difficult to re-establish your credit after bankruptcy
- Bankruptcy may limit your job options
- Bankruptcy stays on your credit record at least 7 years

It Makes sense when:

- It becomes impossible for you to meet your minimum monthly payments.
- The seizure of your salary threatens your job and livelihood.
- Your personal and financial lives are out of control.

Consider bankruptcy when:

- You cannot meet your financial commitments as they fall due.
- You can not realistically expect to be able to catch up with your debt payments in the next 3-5 years
- All you think about is your inability to pay your debts.
- Financial problems seriously interfere with your personal life.

Credit counselling

You cannot sleep at night and the state of your finances threatens your family life and your job. You have decided to do something about it. What next?

Credit counselling services are available in most centres and offer a "free" consulting service. They hold themselves out to be "non-profit" organizations that help consumers decide on the best course of action. Most will offer to negotiate a debt reduction and repayment plan with creditors for you.

Although they are registered as "not for profit"

organizations, obviously they have to be getting money from somewhere in order to stay in operation. They earn most of their money from the spread between what they negotiate with your creditors and the amount that you pay. If you are capable of negotiating with your creditors yourself you might be able to get a better deal than what the credit counseling services will offer you. However most people are uncomfortable with this and prefer to have a third party involved.

There is a disturbing new type of "credit counseling" that has sprung up in Canada in recent years, that seeks to prey on people in desperate situations. I have received several unsolicited telemarketing calls and pre-recorded messages from some of these organizations asking if I would like to avoid paying some of my debts (duh! who wouldn't). I was curious to see what they were up to so I responded to a few. I was told that to qualify I would have to have a minimum amount of debt and be willing to stop making all credit payments for 3 months and redirect that money to them as a "donation" to their "non-profit" organization.

"But wouldn't that ruin my credit rating?" I asked.

"We can always fix that later." replied the telemarketer.

He went on to explain that those 3 months of non-payments would scare my creditors into settling for a much lower amount, or low payments with little or no interest.

"Why would my creditors give in so easily, especially my creditors holding collateral, such as my house or my car?" I asked.

"Let us worry about that." was the reply.

Don't fall for these kinds of offers that are too good to be true. Save your money and negotiate a repayment plan directly with your creditors.

If a repayment plan is not realistic in your case you should see a bankruptcy trustee. Trustees are listed in your local telephone yellow pages under "Bankruptcy Trustees."

If you are considering bankruptcy, call to set up an appointment for free consultations with a couple of different trustees. The first consultation is always free because it is a chance for you to discuss your unique situation with a trained professional. Trustee fees vary somewhat (within ranges prescribed by the Bankruptcy and Insolvency Act) and so does the way they handle different situations, such as whether they will take away your car or let you keep it. Discuss your options before you sign anything.

Meeting with the bankruptcy trustee

A trustee's first duty is, if at all possible, to avoid bankruptcy for you. Bring all your papers. The trustee will see if there is some way of negotiating payments that the creditors will accept. If there is a way, a proposal will be put together that will include payments to your creditors as long as they agree to stop any legal action and phone calls.

Proposals in bankruptcy work as long as the creditors agree to a reduced amount and monthly payments. The trustee will handle calling your creditors or contacting them by letter. You have to keep up the payments under the proposal if you want to keep being protected from your creditors. The debt load should be no more than what you can pay in three to five years. Otherwise, the trustee will recommend bankruptcy.

Declaring bankruptcy

If you and the trustee both agree that bankruptcy is the only alternative because either the debt load is too heavy or because a key creditor refuses to accept the trustee's proposal, you will sign a document that says you are declaring bankruptcy.

Trustee's fee

It is customary for you to pay the trustee's fee at this point. This fee will range from $2,000 in a simple case to many thousands if the trustee thinks it will be complicated and drawn out. The trustee may accept payments from you over a number of months to pay for the trustee's fee.

Cash for everything

The trustee will explain your obligation to not apply for nor obtain credit while your bankruptcy is being settled. If someone offers you credit, you are obligated to state you are a bankrupt in process. You will have to pay cash for everything. This is probably a good thing. Although it will be a tough adjustment at first, paying cash for everything forces you to learn to live within your means. The ability to manage your cash will help you manage your credit later.

The first meeting of creditors

Next, you will attend your first meeting of creditors hosted by the trustee. Creditors usually do not attend the first meeting of creditors unless they are disputing the amount listed in the bankruptcy papers or are concerned about their collateral. If subsequent meetings of creditors are necessary, the trustee will set those up to clear up any misunderstandings or disputes about documentation. They are rarely required. Ninety percent of personal bankruptcies require only the one mandatory meeting of creditors and often no one but the bankrupt individual and the trustee actually show up.

After the first meeting of creditors

The trustee reviews all the creditors' claims over the next few months following the first meeting of creditors. The trustee will then sell your assets and distribute the money from the sale of your assets to your creditors.

Winding up your bankruptcy

The money gets distributed to creditors in the following order:

- Secured creditors (those with collateral)
- Preferred creditors (the trustee's fee is at the top of the list)
- Unsecured creditors (all the rest)

Secured creditors

The secured creditors are paid out of the funds collected from the sale of their collateral. If the sale falls short of the debt, the balance remaining after the sale of the collateral becomes unsecured.

If a particular creditor repossesses its collateral in lieu of payment, the debt less the market value of the collateral becomes an unsecured debt.

Preferred creditors

After the secured creditors are paid out of the proceeds from the sale of their collateral, the preferred creditors are paid in full before any money is paid to anyone else.

Preferred creditors include bankruptcy trustees, funeral homes, and others, as listed in the Bankruptcy and Insolvency Act.

Unsecured creditors

Once all the preferred and secured claims are satisfied, the remaining money, if any is left over, is distributed pro rata to unsecured creditors. This is rarely the case because if there was enough money to pay everyone, there would not be any need for bankruptcy proceedings in the first place.

You may have heard the expression "getting 2 cents on the dollar", what this means is that unsecured creditors are getting about 2 % of what they are owed. The reality is that any payout to unsecured creditors is rare which is why unsecured creditors are usually willing to settle for anything they can get.

Discharging your debts

Once all the assets are sold and all the funds have been distributed, the trustee will apply to the courts to "discharge" your debts to wind up your bankruptcy proceedings. Discharging your debts means that the court erases the balances owed to your creditors in your bankruptcy.

The final bankruptcy hearing

There will be a final hearing in court which you may or may not be asked to attend. The bankruptcy judge has a large amount of discretion in dealing with each bankruptcy case.

If you are asked to attend, the court will take the opportunity to remind you not to do this again. The judge can decide to delay discharging your debts to force you to live within your means (remember you cannot have credit until you are discharged from your debts).

The judge will appoint a financial advisor to give you financial counselling and report back to the court to make sure you will not get yourself back in the same situation. This is done for your own protection as well as that of your future creditors.

The court can choose to not discharge a particular debt and order you to pay that debt before the other debts are discharged.

Family support payments and student loans

Some debts, such as family support payments and student loans less than 7 years old, are not discharged in a bankruptcy. You will still have to pay these after the bankruptcy.

Government taxes

A few years ago, if you owed income taxes, the government used to be a preferred creditor, but now the law says the government is just another unsecured creditor. This change discourages the government from being overzealous in seizing assets, knowing that it will have to relinquish them in a bankruptcy. In the past, as a preferred creditor, the government had first call after the trustee on any and all assets that were not already collateral, so tax collectors would "encourage" people who owed back taxes to seek bankruptcy protection, even if that was not necessarily the best solution for the taxpayer and the taxpayer's other creditors.

Discharge date

At the bankruptcy hearing, the judge sets the date on which your debts will be erased (this is called the discharge date). Shortly after that date, the trustee will send you documents confirming your debts are erased.

After the discharge date, you are free to rebuild your financial life and your credit without the crushing burden of your previous monthly payments.

The effect of bankruptcy on your credit

Bankruptcy is an item that is part of the public record. The credit bureaus regularly review these public bankruptcy records in order to add these items to the credit reports of the people who are bankrupt. It is impossible to escape detection and not have your bankruptcy appear on your credit report.

A bankruptcy will stay on your credit report for a minimum of seven years. A second bankruptcy will stay on your credit report for fourteen years. A third bankruptcy might never come off.

Many creditors will be reluctant to grant credit to you if you have been recently discharged. After bankruptcy, your credit score will plummet or disappear altogether. So plan on living on cash for a while. As time wears on and your discharge date fades further and further into the past, your chances of credit approval will start to increase again.

Alternatives to bankruptcy

There is always an alternative to bankruptcy. The question is whether or not that alternative makes more sense than bankruptcy.

Consumer proposal

In Canada, Division 1, Part 3 of the Bankruptcy and Insolvency Act allows for a plan called a "consumer proposal". Creditors who have submitted acceptable claims to the bankruptcy trustee can vote on the proposal by proxy or in person at the creditors' meeting.

Creditors must agree

Section 54 (d) of the Bankruptcy and Insolvency Act states:

"The proposal shall be deemed to be accepted by the creditors if, and only if, all classes of unsecured creditors vote for the acceptance of the proposal by a majority in number and two thirds in value of the unsecured creditors of each class present, personally or by proxy, at the meeting and voting on the resolution."

In other words, the majority (greater than fifty percent) of unsecured creditors who represent at least two thirds of the money owed must vote in favour of accepting the proposal.

The effect of a consumer proposal on your credit

Because it is a matter of public record, your credit report will show that a consumer proposal repayment plan has been put in place. This is not good for your credit report because a notice of a consumer proposal repayment plan will lower your credit score but not as much as if you have a series of R9's or a couple of judgements. This will severely limit your ability to get credit for a couple of years even after you successfully follow through on all your payments. However, it will show your bills as paid when everything is finished.

The final decision

If you are considering bankruptcy get advice and price quotes from a couple of different bankruptcy trustees. They may tell you what you already know and suggest that you get a part-time job, sell your car, stick to a budget and pay everybody off.

It is a tough decision to make. Most people feel a tremendous sense of relief after declaring bankruptcy and realizing that the whole process is not all that frightening after all. However, the final decision is yours. You will be living with the consequences of your decision for a long time.

"Creditors have better memories than debtors."

Benjamin Franklin

12

Dealing with Creditors

Don't ignore your mail

It is common for people who are in financial trouble to stop opening any mail that looks like a bill. Resist this temptation.

I had a friend call me to ask for help. Money had been taken from his bank account. When he contacted his bank for an explanation, he was told that a court order had arrived demanding that the bank remit the balance in his bank account to the court. He called the telephone number on the court order and was told by the court that this item was a garnishee of his bank account pursuant to a judgment.

My friend then called me and asked how a creditor could do something like that. He had not gone to court for anything. I asked him if he remembered not paying a debt. He admitted that he was behind on a few bills, but was adamant that no one had taken him to court. He explained that he hated receiving repetitive annoying collection letters. So after a while, he stopped opening anything that even looked like a bill. He had a box full of unopened mail.

After getting a few more details, I figured out what must have happened. Unable to collect, the creditor had issued a statement of claim and had served my friend by mail. He had not bothered to open the envelope. After the mandatory waiting period, the creditor filed a default judgment. A default judgment means that the court agrees the money is owed because no statement of defence was filed by the defendant. A copy of the judgment was mailed by the court to my friend, but he did not open that letter either. A default judgment also gives the creditor the right to seize assets belonging to the debtor in order to get paid. I suggested to my friend that he settle this bill immediately before his wages were seized. He did.

Your creditors can collect the debt by assigning your debt to a collection agency, or press on to judgment and garnishee (seizing your bank account and wages). They may even temporarily ignore your debt. However, one thing is certain, you still owe the money and, sooner or later, your creditors will take action.

An unexpected drop in income

A temporary illness or job loss may make it impossible for you to pay your bills on time. Whatever the situation, if you find that you cannot make your payments, contact your creditors at once. Try to work out a modified payment plan that reduces the payments to a manageable level for you.

Call your creditors immediately

If you have paid promptly in the past, your creditors will be willing to work with you. Do not wait until your account is turned over to a collection agency. By the time that a creditor finally decides to turn your account over to a collection agency they have given up on you. They figure that you are not going to pay and so they stop trying to collect and finally decide to let a third party, such as a collection agency, continue the effort. The collection agency charges your creditor anywhere from a quarter to a half of what they are able to collect from you. The creditor figures that if the collection agency manages to collect anything, it will be a bonus (perhaps a miracle), so they are happy to pay the commission. Your creditor then proceeds to write off the balance on your account to bad debt.

Plan ahead for the possibility of a loss of income

Everyone needs to set aside at least three months worth of monthly payments to reduce the financial hardship created by a temporary illness or job loss. Unused credit card limits will work while you start saving, but it takes discipline not to use the available credit. A three month cushion that will cover your monthly obligations such as rent or mortgage payments, credit card and loan payments, and any other payments that you need to make each and every month is the absolute minimum; six months or a year's worth should be your goal.

Ignoring your creditors reduces your credit score

When your creditor gives up on you and decides to turn the account over to a collection agency they also send a notice to the credit bureaus that your account is now a bad debt and assign it the worst rating, an R-9. This rating hurts your credit score. The collection agency in turn also tells the credit bureaus they have a collection item for you. The collection agency notice also hurts your credit score.

Out of the frying pan into the fire

A client called me to ask for advice about collecting a debt that he was owed. He asked me if I would call his client since French was her first language and it was also mine. I agreed. I managed to get her on the phone, but she refused to discuss the debt or make any arrangements for repayment. I told her that my client was prepared to sue. She said that she did not care and would not pay.

Since this was a relatively small debt the action would go through Small Claims court. A copy of the Statement of Claim, a document submitted to the court that says how much is owed and why the money is owed, was mailed to her. What she should have done at this point was to file a defence. Instead she ignored the document. Therefore, a default judgment was filed in favour of the creditor.

In an attempt to locate her assets, bank accounts, vehicles, etc. she was sent a subpoena to appear at a judgement debtor examination. She ignored this as well. At this point I called her to confirm that she had received all these documents. She acknowledged that she had, but was refusing to do anything about it.

Next, the court issued a summons ordering her to appear at a show cause hearing to explain why she had failed to appear at the judgement debtor examination. This document was served in person. She ignored the summons and did not show up in court.

Ignoring a Judge's summons is the wrong thing to do. Big mistake! The judge ruled that she was in contempt and issued a warrant for her arrest. When the police appeared at her door she refused to open it. They are now in the process of getting a court order to break the door down and arrest her using force.

The stupidity of this whole matter is that nothing would have happened to her if she had simply talked to her creditor. There is no such thing as a debtor's prison in Canada. Had she not ignored the letters and court documents and had appeared in court, both the creditor and the court would have agreed to any reasonable arrangement. All she had to say was that although she wanted to pay, she had no money. The court would simply have looked at her finances and agreed to some ridiculously small monthly payment. However, instead she is facing criminal charges and the prospect of being arrested and spending some time in jail. The point of this story is to remind you not to ignore your creditors.

Settling a debt with an unsecured creditor

If you are in serious financial trouble but want to avoid bankruptcy, you can try to settle with your creditors. Most unsecured debts can be settled for less than the balance. An unsecured debt is a debt where there is no collateral. Examples are department store credit cards, unsecured bank credit cards, personal loans, amounts remaining after a foreclosure or repossession, returned cheques and medical bills.

However, the more your creditor is in a "monopoly" position where the creditor is virtually the only source of the product or service that you need now and that you will continue to need in the future, such as utility companies, the less likely that creditor will settle for less than the full balance. Unsecured creditors will usually take an amount less than the balance as a final settlement in full to close a troublesome account because they realize that they will probably get nothing if there is a bankruptcy.

Settling a debt with a secured creditor

Collateralized debts, such as home or automobile loans, are much more difficult to settle. If a secured creditor can simply repossess the collateral, sell it, and get the money to pay the balance, why negotiate with you? Trying to negotiate a settlement while you still possess the creditor's collateral seldom works. Your creditor must believe that it is in their best interest to settle with you. The reality is that settling a debt with a secured creditor is difficult, nearly impossible.

Car loans

If your creditor thinks that you are in more trouble than you let on, your creditor may make a "pre-emptive strike" by repossessing the collateral in order to prevent its deterioration or it being sold without their permission.

This is especially true with car loans. Your lender may demand the car back if they believe that you do not have the money to spend on maintenance, for example, thereby letting the car and its value deteriorate.

The same holds true for the mortgage company if they believe that you are letting your home become run down. The mortgage company will be worried about a reduction in your home's market value because you cannot afford the maintenance.

Making an offer

When you contact your creditors, you have to be prepared to offer a settlement. Make sure that you can afford what you are offering. If you do not follow through on your commitment, your creditor will be unlikely to give you a second chance.

The settlement agreement

Never expect your creditor or your creditor's collection agency to honour an agreement that was only made verbally. It is not that they will not, but it is difficult to prove later who said what over the telephone. Everything must be in writing and, even then, you may have to make your creditor or your creditor's collection agency live up to its end of the bargain by being very persistent.

Essentials of the settlement agreement

The following items should be in your written agreement:

• The amount of the expected payment along with the confirmation of which debt is being paid and how it is being paid.

• A confirmation that this amount settles the debt in full and that no further action will be taken.

• A commitment from your creditor or your creditor's collection agency to authorize the credit bureaus to remove any mention of this negative item.

Getting the negative item removed

A written commitment from your creditor or your creditor's collection agency to remove the negative item is intended to prevent future inquiries from showing any record of the collection action. Every creditor who reports to the credit bureau can also change the information they report. The key for you is to make sure you communicate directly with someone who has that authority.

Once you get the agreement in writing, you should pay promptly. Do not give your creditor or your creditor's collection agency a chance to change their mind. Write the phrase "full and final settlement" on both the front and back of your cheque. Make sure you also write on your cheque your account number or file number. This will insure that your payment will be credited to your account.

Larger creditors, such as major credit card companies, large department stores, or banks, will require more perseverance on your part before they will agree to delete a negative item, but virtually every creditor will give in with the right amount of coaxing. I cannot stress enough the importance of getting your creditor or your creditor's collection agency to agree in writing to remove the negative item from your credit report before you pay. You will not have any leverage afterward.

Making the harassment stop

Dodging collection calls only delays the inevitable and makes matters worse. It makes the collector work harder and therefore less likely to negotiate a payment plan with you when they finally get a hold of you.

Call collectors first

The most effective way you can prevent being harassed by collectors is to call them first. Present a proposal for payment. Collectors will be much more receptive if you are contacting them first instead of the other way around. It is always the person making the call who has the advantage by being ready and making the call on their schedule. If you make a commitment to keep in touch regularly and you follow through on that commitment, you will be in control and eliminate those annoying calls.

The easiest way to make the collection calls stop is to make a payment arrangement and stick to it. The key is to negotiate an arrangement that you are capable of sticking to. Don't tell the collector that you will make a payment of $100 on Tuesday if you know that you get paid on Wednesday and that the most you can afford to give them is $30. But what is you really have no money to give them? Tell them the truth. Tell them when you expect to have money, and schedule a followuw-up phone call. Of course they are going to try to bully you into paying them the full amount, collection agencies get paid a percentage of what they are able to collect.

When you are feeling intimidated by telephone collectors I think it is helpful to remember that generally the people making the collection calls are no different than the average person and many of them have financial problems of their own. The technique that they use of not giving their first name (hello this is Mr. Jones from ....) while calling you by your first name is intended to intimidate you into thinking you are dealing with a "superior" like your teacher in elementary school. Ignore it, Mr. Jones is probably just someone like the kid down the street and this is his first job and he can't stand it. The turnover rate for telephone collectors is very high.

The rules about collection calls

In Canada, the Collection Agencies Act, regulated by the provinces, governs collection practices. It limits what a collection agency can do to collect from you.

Consumer collections

The Collection Agencies Act rules apply only to a collector calling a consumer for a personal debt. These rules do not apply if a collector is calling a small business owner for a bill incurred by the business.

Hours

The Collection Agencies Act says that collectors cannot "harass" you. This means that a collector cannot call you at work. It also says that a collector cannot call you at home after 9 p.m. or before 7 a.m. nor on Sundays nor on statutory holidays. However, a collector can call a cellular telephone number anytime.

Calling your employer

Even if your creditor or your creditor's collection agency is preparing to seize (also called "garnishee") your wages, the only reason a collector is permitted to call your employer is to verify employment or to ask for a home telephone number and address. The employer is not obligated in any way to provide the information to the collector.

Keeping your personal information private

The collector needs to be careful not to divulge to your employer any of your private information, including any details such as the nature or the amount of the debt. Otherwise, both the collector and the collection agency can be liable for any damage they cause to you by discussing these matters with your employer.

The obligations of creditors under PIPEDA

PIPEDA stands for "Personal Information Protection and Electronic Data Act" of Canada. It was created to "govern the collection, use and disclosure of personal information in a manner that recognizes the right of privacy of individuals with respect to their personal information and the need of organizations to collect, use or disclose personal information for purposes that a reasonable person would consider appropriate in the circumstances." In other words, the act tries to balance the need for individual privacy with the need of businesses to have some private information such as your mailing address, etc.

With PIPEDA, a business requires an individual's permission to collect, use, and disclose, any personal information.

Specifically, it requires businesses to tell individuals what personal information is in their records so that you can verify its accuracy and have a chance to correct it. This means that creditors have an obligation under PIPEDA to tell you what is in their files about you. PIPEDA requires that companies must have the most accurate information available.

Every company must appoint a PIPEDA information officer who is accountable for enforcing the provisions of this privacy legislation. You can contact the information officer who has an obligation to assist you in obtaining and correcting the information the company has on you.

Telling the collector to stop calling

Persistent, unwarranted, repetitive calling, especially at unreasonable hours, is harassment. Under the Collection Agencies Act, a collector must stop calling you if you instruct them to stop. The collector is obligated to stop calling you as long as you provide a mailing address for correspondence. If you do not supply a mailing address, the collector has a right to continue calling you at home. It is a good idea to confirm in writing to your creditor or your creditor's collection agency your request for them to stop calling.

Although you can stop getting collection telephone calls, you cannot prevent your creditor or your creditor's collection agency from taking you to court. Once you have given your mailing address to your creditor or your creditor's collection agency, they can serve you at that address if a statement of claim is issued against you in a court action. You can get the collectors to stop calling you, but they will then have little choice but to start court proceedings, sometimes it is better to put up with a few telephone calls.

If the harassment continues

The provincial governments license collection agencies. So if a collector continues to call and harass you, you can file a complaint with the governing body that issues licenses to collection agencies in your province. It is that governing body's duty to investigate all complaints. If it receives too many complaints about a particular collection agency, the governing body can decide not to renew a collection agency's license, or even revoke it. Sometimes, just threatening to complain to the registrar is enough to make them stop calling.

Personal vs. business debt

The gloves are pretty much off where business collections are concerned. A collector can call a business telephone number at any time. If you are a sole proprietor, a collector can call you at home to discuss a bill owed by your business.

On the other hand, if a collector is calling you about a personal debt that has nothing to do with your business, such as a personal utility bill, then the rules governing personal collections apply.

The rules get a little fuzzy when you are a sole proprietor. When the only source of funds to pay your personal bills is your business, a case can be made that the personal bill a collector is trying to resolve is really a business issue because the business ultimately pays for it. A collector paid on commission will do whatever it takes to get the money. As a sole proprietor, you are vulnerable in this situation. You will have to talk to the collector and make a deal if you do not want to keep getting the calls.

"Tricks and treachery are the practice of fools, that don't have brains enough to be honest. "

Benjamin Franklin

Identity Theft 13

You are at the store picking up a couple of items on the way home. You hand over your credit card to the clerk. You get ready to sign the slip. The clerk turns to you and quietly says, "Sir, sorry, but your card has been declined. How do you want to pay for this?" You know that your credit card bill is paid in full. You tell the clerk, "This must be a mistake. Please try again."

The store clerk tries again with the same result. No problem. You pull out your bank debit card. It too is declined. You ask the clerk to retry that one as well. Again, same result. So you pull out your last twenty-dollar bill and pay cash for the items. You thank the clerk and leave the store determined to find out what is going on.

When you get home, you immediately get on the phone to the credit card company. To your surprise, the credit card company informs you that your card has been frozen. You have exceeded your credit limit. You don't understand. The balance is paid and you did not make any purchases. You are told that you have purchased several items lately and that you have exceeded your credit limit. You deny making those purchases. You ask to speak to the manager, but you are asked for your password first before you are allowed to discuss any details about your account with the manager. You give your password, but are told it is not correct. Strange! You do not recall changing the password. The manager says that he will investigate and contact you by mail. He follows the usual procedure and confirms your mailing address. It is different! So he says he will call you back at home. When he verifies the number, it too is different! So you ask the manager to call you at your correct number. He promises to call you back after he has looked into the matter. You hang up hoping this is simply a mistake that will be corrected shortly.

Next, you call your bank to see why your debit card did not work. Again, your password is incorrect and no one will discuss your account with you over the phone. They invite you to come to the bank to discuss it in person.

When you get to the bank, you are ushered into an office and asked for ID before proceeding. You pull out some picture ID and they see that you are who you say you are. They are now able to discuss the account with you.

Bad news! Your account has only three dollars and twenty-seven cents left in it.

"But I had over two thousand dollars in it this morning!" You reply.

"Sorry, sir, but that account had most of that money withdrawn from it this morning."

"How?" You ask.

"From what I can tell, it was a withdrawal using your bank card at an automated teller." the bank employee replied.

"I didn't do that!" you scream.

"Sir, you are responsible for your card and what is done with it. The money is gone from your account."

A terrifying thought crosses your mind.

"Check my savings account. I have over $4000 in it."

"Nothing in there." The bank employee tells you.

"My credit card has purchases I didn't make." you add.

"I don't want to alarm you, but it sounds like you may be a victim of identity theft. Shall I call the police for you?"

A growing trend

Sadly, identity theft is quickly becoming a much more common experience than most people realize. According to research done by the CPP Group for the Institute of Credit Management in the U.K., "The average time that people believe it would take to realize they are victims of identity theft is 103 days, far short of the actual time of 480 days (16 months).

People also underestimate how long it would take to set things straight again. According to the same research, "One third of those questioned claimed they had no idea how long it might take to reclaim their identity, while the average time estimated was 127 hours, far short of the actual average time of 300 hours."

In North America, it is estimated that half of the identity theft cases involve someone you know (relatives, friends, coworkers).

Opportunities for identity theft

You are at a restaurant and the bill arrives at the table. You look it over. It seems fine. You put your credit card in the tray along with the bill and your server picks up the tray and says he will be right back. A few moments later, your card is returned to you and you sign your bill and you put away your card. This is a very normal experience for most people.

However, in those few moments when it was out of your sight, your card could have been swept through a reader that scans all the personal information on your card. That is all the identity thieves need to start the ball rolling.

Stealing your identity

Identity thieves can have the mailing address for your credit card statement and PIN numbers changed within moments of accessing your credit card information. Then they can access your credit report file, driver's permit information, and all other personal information about you.

Do not think it cannot happen to you: it has already happened to millions of people around the world.

Keeping track of identity theft

According to the Federal Trade Commission in the U.S.:

"Between January and December 2003, Consumer Sentinel, the complaint database developed and maintained by the FTC, received over half of a million consumer fraud and identity theft complaints. Consumers reported losses from fraud of more than $400 million."

The Sentinel database contains over a million complaints.

Keeping it quiet

You don't hear too much about this because the credit industry wants to keep cases of identity theft out of the news. If consumers lose confidence in the credit industry's ability to safeguard their sensitive personal information, companies dependent on the credit industry will see their profits drop.

What should I do if it happens to me?

If you are a victim of identity theft, you have to act quickly. As you go through the necessary steps, remember that all communication should be in writing. Even if you call because of the urgency to notify parties such as the credit bureaus and the bank, follow up in writing to confirm your conversations.

Keep a written record

A written record of transactions, dates, and

conversations might be crucial later in proving you did what you say you did, when you said you did it. If a credit card company takes you to court for a bill that the identity thief incurred, it might take your written record to prove to the court that you should not have to pay.

Call the police

Contact the police immediately. Always ask for a copy of the police report and keep it in your files. This will establish a useful paper trail that will be vital to defending yourself successfully in any court actions. Keep the phone number of your investigator handy and give it to your creditors and others who require verification.

Notify the credit bureaus

Immediately after you have made a report to the police report the theft to Equifax and TransUnion. When you believe you are a victim of identity theft, any one bureau that you notify has an obligation to notify the other one. However, I strongly recommend that you notify each of the credit bureaus yourself. Do it by telephone followed up with a written notice by certified mail or courier so that you have proof of such notice.

Tagging your credit file

Tell the credit bureaus that you believe someone other than you is using your personal identifying information. The credit bureaus will tag your file with a special alert warning so that any credit bureau member or lender inquiring on your file will be notified of the possible fraudulent use of your identifying information.

Confirm the fraud warning is on your credit report

Ask each credit bureau in writing to provide you with a copy of your credit report so that you can see for yourself that the fraud notice is in place. It will stay on your credit report for five years. The fraud warning requires creditors to confirm your identity before extending credit. This is important because the thieves may decide to try again once they figure the heat is off.

Keep a copy of all documents, including all letters and copies of your credit report. It is vital evidence in any future court action. Ask each of the credit bureaus for the contact information for each credit grantor that has opened accounts for your stolen identity, as well as the contact information for each credit bureau member that made credit inquiries.

Remove unauthorized inquiries

Find out how many credit inquiries have been generated due to the fraudulent access. Ask the credit bureaus in writing that these inquiries be removed and make sure that you confirm by looking at your credit report yourself.

Monitor new inquiries

For at least 2 years, order a copy of your credit report every month or so to monitor any new inquiries.

Credit cards

If you have existing credit cards and other credit accounts, get replacement cards using new account numbers. It is wise to add new passwords to your accounts whenever possible. Make sure you do not use your mother's maiden name or other easy-to-guess passwords such as your birthday or address.

Collection calls

If debt collectors start calling asking you to pay unpaid bills on fraudulent credit accounts, ask for the name of the company, the name of the person contacting you, their phone number, and their address. Tell the collector that you are a victim of fraud and are not responsible for the account. Ask the collector for the name and contact information for the referring credit issuer, the amount of the debt, account number, and dates of the invoices.

Get it writing

Follow up in writing to the debt collector explaining your situation. Ask that the collection agency confirm in writing that you do not owe the debt and that the account has been closed.

Bank

If your bank information or your bank cheques were stolen, put stop payments on any outstanding cheques. Cancel your chequing and savings accounts and obtain new account numbers. Give the bank a secret password for your account.

Debit card

If your debit card has been stolen or compromised, report it immediately. Get a new card, account number, and password. Do not use your old password.

Monitor your bank accounts

Read your account statements carefully. You may be liable if fraud is not reported quickly. Be sure to read the debit card contract for time and liability limits. These limits can vary from card to card.

No one is immune to debit card fraud

It happened to me in July of 2005, during my first book tour across Canada. I was in Calgary putting in a long day of television and radio appearances informing people how to protect themselves from identity theft. As usual, that evening my wife checked our bank account via the Internet.

"Did you take any money out of the bank today?" she asked.

"Of course not. You were with me all day." I replied.

"Well its all gone! Everything in the bank account is gone!" she screamed.

The sense of panic that we felt was incredible. There we were on the other side of the country, and suddenly our bank account was empty. At this point it was obvious that we had been victims of identity theft but didn't yet know the extent of the problem.

It turns out that my bank debit card had been duplicated, along with about 3000 other bank cards, as a result of using it to pay for gas at a gas station in Toronto about 2 months previously.

The bank told me that they could see (although I could not) that the thieves had made numerous inquiries on my account at automated teller machines during that time. They chose that particular day to strike presumably because most of the victims account balances were at their highest point of the month (pay days, other deposits etc.).

What happened was that someone placed a tiny recording device on the cable between the debit machine and the computer/cash register. These tiny devices are virtually unnoticeable and collect the card information as well as the PIN number that you enter. They can steal the information from thousands of cards, and when it is full the thief removes the device, connects it to a computer, and creates clones of the original cards, and the windfall begins.

For this to happen the card never has to leave your hand, and no one needs to be looking over your shoulder to see your PIN number.

Fortunately for me, I had stopped in at a local bank branch in Calgary that morning and had spoken to the manager about an unrelated matter, and had appeared on Calgary television that day, and then had used my debit card to pay for some items at a convenience store in Calgary that afternoon just prior to my account being cleaned out at a bank machine in Toronto. So it was obvious that I couldn't be in both Toronto and Calgary at the same time, and therefore my card had been cloned. Also, fortunately for me, the size of this fraud was huge, the number of people who had been victimized at the same time by using the same gas station made it obvious that a crime had been committed.

In this case, the bank reimbursed me for the stolen money, it was back in my bank account the following morning, but they did not have to. If you carefully read your debit card agreement you will see that you are responsible for any losses that result from the unauthorized use of your PIN number.

A few months later, back in Ottawa, I interviewed two Ottawa police fraud investigators who told me that this type of crime has become very prevalent and that regardless of the preventative steps the banks take the crooks are always two steps ahead.

From that point on, I have never used my debit card to make a purchase at a gas station, or a convenience store, anywhere where there is a high volume of transactions and a high turnover of staff. For these sorts of purchases it is safer to use a credit card or pay cash.

Change of address

If you suspect an identity thief has filed a change of address with the post office, notify the local postmaster. You may also need to talk with the mail carrier. Be on the lookout for any mail forwarding changes. Inform the police if someone else has filled out a false change of address for your mail.

Telephone

Your telephone and cell phone accounts can be stolen. Set up a password for changing your local and long distance accounts. If your telephone calling card has been stolen or if there are fraudulent charges on your telephone account, cancel your card immediately and open a new account. Again, ask the police and the telephone company to provide you reports in writing.

Driver's licence and vehicle ownership

You may need to change your driver's license number if someone is using yours as ID to write bad cheques or for other types of fraud. Call the driver's licence office to see if another license was issued in your name. Request and get a new number.

Using your car as collateral for a loan

Someone posing as you trying to get a loan using your car as collateral would probably not be successful in having a lien put on it without your knowledge. Any creditor taking a lien on your car for a loan will first want to match the serial number on the current plate number ownership certificate to the serial number that is physically on your car's dashboard, door or motor. As long as you are in possession of your car, that should not happen. However, if the identity thief is someone who has access to your car it certainly is possible.

Insurance

Contact your insurance company immediately by telephone. Follow up in writing to update them on the situation. If your insurance company gets a claim from the thief, ask them to contact you and the police.

Civil litigation

If a civil judgment is entered in your name for your

identity thief's actions, contact the court where the judgment was entered and report that you are a victim of identity theft.

Sometimes victims of identity theft are wrongfully accused of crimes committed by the identity thief. For example using your drivers' license to get away with speeding. If this happens to you it is definitely time to get a lawyer and start defending yourself.

Using a deceased person's ID

If a deceased relative's information is being used to perpetrate identity theft, or if you personally know the identity thief, call the police immediately. If a deceased relative's information is being used, follow the same procedures as if it was your own.

Bills that are not yours

Do not pay any bill or portion of a bill that is a result of fraud. Do not cover any cheques that were written or cashed fraudulently. Your credit rating will be affected, but only temporarily. If any company or collection agency suggests otherwise, restate your willingness to cooperate, but do not allow yourself to be coerced into paying fraudulent bills.

Birth certificate

Your birth certificate is proof of your identity. It is an important way to prove your name, age and where you were born. You need a birth certificate to apply for most government documents and services, including drivers' licences, passports, and social benefits.

Reporting a stolen birth certificate

The law says that you must immediately report a lost, stolen, destroyed, or found birth certificate right away. By cancelling lost or stolen birth certificates, the government wants to make that sure no criminal can use the stolen birth certificate to commit fraud or identity theft.

Protecting your documents

In addition to names, addresses and phone numbers, thieves look for documents containing social insurance numbers, drivers licence numbers, credit card and banking information, bankcards, calling cards, birth certificates and passports.

When you are not traveling, store your birth certificate in a safe place, along with other valuable documents, including your passport, and shred them after they expire.

Review your monthly statements

Review the balances on your statements from banks, credit cards and companies regularly and report any discrepancies right away. If your bills do not arrive, or you applied for a new credit card that has not arrived, call the credit grantor immediately.

Leaving on vacation

If you are going to be away from home, ask a trusted neighbour to pick up your mail, or go to your local post office (with identification) and ask for the post office's "hold mail" service. Carry as few cards and documents as possible.

Keep a close eye on your credit cards

Always check to see that the credit card you get back is your own. Waiters may be dealing with several bills at once and I have, on more than one occasion, been handed someone else's card by mistake.

Protect your personal information

Be wary of giving out any personal information over the telephone unless you have placed the call yourself or know the business. Never tell anyone the password you use at the Automated Banking Machine, and be sure no one is watching when you use an ABM.

If it's too good to be true . . .

Chain letters and false investment schemes try to win your confidence with promises of incredible returns, but often, they are only after your personal and credit information.

Fraudulent Internet sites

Fake or "spoof" web sites are designed to trick consumers and collect their personal information. Be cautious when clicking on a link or an unknown web site or unfamiliar email. The link may take you to a fraudulent site. Be wary of computer start-up software that asks for registration information. Never share your computer passwords.

No personal information via email

Do not use email to send personal information.

Discourage harvesting of your email address - think about creating "disposable" email addresses for online purchases, mask your address, or use a unique email address. Beware of Internet promotions that ask for personal information. Identity thieves may use false offers to get you to give them your information. After completing any sort of financial transaction online, make sure you sign out of the web site and clear your Internet file/cache. Most financial institutions provide instructions on how to clear the caches under their "security" section.

Credit card purchases

Do not give a credit card number or other identification information to a company that does not provide their name, business address, telephone number and email address. Before giving your credit card number or other financial information to a business, make sure that their web site is protected and secured. If you are buying something over the Internet using your credit card, look for the lock symbol located somewhere on the browser.

If you make a lot of on-line purchases, consider having a second credit card with a lower credit limit from a separate financial institution that you use exclusively for this purpose.

Minimum personal information on your cheques

When you are ordering cheques from your bank, use initials and last name on your cheques instead of your full name. Do not put your home telephone number on your cheques. If you are asked to put a telephone number on your cheque before it will be accepted, use your work number.

Pay cash when you can

Obviously, paying cash for your purchases reduces the opportunities for thieves to steal your identity, assuming of course that you got the cash from a secure ATM. I am very reluctant to use the private cash machines that are located in convenience stores and bars. Aside from the fact that they charge higher fees than bank ATM's, they could potentially provide a vehicle for thieves who want to clone cards.

No obvious passwords

Of course, you should not use obvious passwords such as birthdays, addresses, telephone numbers, etc.

Stolen wallet or computer

If your wallet or computer is stolen, even if it is returned to you seemingly intact, do not assume that your information was not stolen. You should cancel all cards and change all passwords.

Keep a list of account numbers and contact info

Make a list of all your important identification documents such as passports, birth certificates, etc. as well as credit card account numbers along with the emergency contact information for each one. Keep them in a safe, separate location (not in your wallet or purse).

Screen names

Teach your children to keep their identities confidential in chat rooms, bulletin boards or newsgroups. Help them learn to choose screen names that do not identity them, and to understand that any information they exchange on the Internet is not private.

Credit monitoring services

Equifax and TransUnion offer "automatic" credit monitoring services. For a yearly fee, an email will be sent to you anytime a new inquiry or a negative item shows up on your report. If anyone is attempting to open accounts in your name this is a great way of catching it early. Using this service does not prevent you from ordering your own credit report at any time as well.

What about "Pre-Paid Legal" services?

I am regularly asked if I would promote various "Pre-Paid Legal" services as a means of protecting yourself from identity theft. I have looked into them and I do not feel comfortable about endorsing them. Perhaps they offer other valuable services, but for identity theft protection for Canadians they are not very useful.

These are generally US companies that offer to provide you with a lawyer to help you in the event that you are a victim, but obviously there is a cap on how much they will cover. The biggest flaw is that they claim to monitor any negative items that show up on your credit report, but the credit reports they use are from Experian and Northern, two companies that are not widely used in Canada. If you are considering signing up read the literature carefully first, make sure that you know exactly what you are getting for your money.

Ten signs that your identity may have been stolen:

1) Bills and statements do not arrive when they are supposed to. They may have been stolen from the mailbox or someone has changed the mailing address.

2) You receive calls from collection agencies or creditors for accounts you do not have. Someone may have opened a new account in your name, or added charges to your account.

3) Financial account statements show withdrawals or transfers you did not make.

4) A lender calls to say you have been approved or denied credit for which you have not applied. Or, you apply for credit and are turned down for reasons that do not make sense, given your financial position.

5) Your renewal form for your driver's licence or car ownership does not arrive.

6) You do not get your yearly insurance renewal forms.

7) You stop getting the annoying offers in the mail that you always used to get.

8) Your yearly income tax form does not arrive.

9) You get telemarketing calls from local businesses welcoming you to the neighbourhood although you have lived there for years.

10) You do not receive your quarterly property tax bill.

Steps to deal with identity theft

If you think that you have been a victim of identity theft, there are steps you should take immediately to minimize damage and help prevent further fraud or theft. Time is critical.

When contacting financial institutions, credit card issuers or other companies that may have provided the identity thief with unauthorized credit, money, goods or services, follow these steps:

1) Contact your creditor's fraud department and ask them to cancel and reissue any card that were effected and close any fraudulent or affected accounts. Explain what has happened and ask them to investigate.

2) If you have any government issued documents such as driver's permit, birth certificate, or passport that might have been duplicated notify the appropriate government office immediately.

3) Report the incident to your local police. Get a police report number and include it in all correspondence with financial institutions, credit issuers, and credit bureaus.

4) Complete an identity theft statement

5) Keep a record of your actions, even after the case has been resolved. Errors can reappear on your credit reports or your information can be re-circulated. If this happens, you'll be glad you kept a written record.

The identity theft statement

An identity theft statement is a form that can be obtained from any major financial institution in Canada. Fill out this form to notify financial institutions, credit card issuers and other companies:

1) That the identity theft occurred
2) That you did not create the debt or charges
3) Gives them the information to begin investigating

Completing an identity theft statement does not guarantee that the identity thief will be prosecuted or that the debt or charges will be cleared.

The identity theft statement consists of two parts.

Part One: Identity Theft Statement

General information about you and the identity theft.

Part Two: Statement of Unauthorized Account Activity

Specific information about accounts or activities. Complete this section specifically for each company you are notifying, and send each company only the information that relates to accounts or activities with that company.

Once you have completed and signed the Identity Theft Statement, attach copies (not originals) of any supporting documents you have (for example, transaction records, receipts, a police report). Keep a copy of everything that you are submitting for your records.

Sending out the Identity Theft Statement

Provide the completed identity theft statement and attached documents to each financial institution, credit card issuer or other company that provided the identity thief with unauthorized credit or money. Send the documents by registered mail or courier, or deliver them in person and get a signature, so that you can prove that they were received.

The companies will review the information and will contact you to let you know the outcome of their investigation, or to obtain further information.

Protect your Identity Theft Statement

The identity theft statement and supporting materials will contain important information about you, so they should be kept in a safe place, and only shared with financial institutions, credit card issuers, other companies and law enforcement agencies that require the information.

Outcome of the investigation

By investigating your identity theft statement, each company will determine whether to absolve you of the debt. Note that, if you are seeking reimbursement for any loss, you may need to provide separate forms or documents, and reimbursement will be subject to applicable policies and account agreements.

The identity theft statement is only intended for companies that give you credit and other services. Do not send the identity theft statement to a government department or ministry.

Who are the thieves?

Sophisticated types of fraud such as cell phone cloning, credit card cloning, debit card cloning and false ID's require technical expertise. Organized crime has discovered how lucrative this sort of fraud can be. Because the payoff can be huge, it is usually organized crime that bankrolls groups who have the technical sophistication to carry out identity theft on a large scale.

However, on a smaller scale, if you find that your debit card has been used to withdraw money from your bank account, or that unauthorized purchases have been made on your credit card, upsetting as it may be, the majority of the time the thief is someone close to you. They are the ones who have the most opportunity. Chances are that the perpetrator is someone with some pressing need for money such as a drug or gambling problem.

Recovery from identity theft takes time and effort

Putting your life together after you have been a victim of identity theft can take a year or more. Getting your government documents replaced can take one to six months. Obtaining replacement cards and re-establishing your credit limits and lines of credit can take a month or more.

Credit card companies should remove any fraudulent bills from your account immediately or tag them as items being investigated for identity fraud.

Losses from identity theft

Unfortunately, you may be stuck with some losses if someone uses your debit card fraudulently. My daughter lost fifteen hundred dollars when her "friend" stole her bank card and withdrew what she had in the bank account. She had peeked once over my daughter's shoulder to get her personal identification number. That money was never recovered. Banks will not replace money stolen by thieves using your bank card to make cash withdrawals from automated banking machines. Your are responsible for your bank card and PIN number until you notify the bank.

You may also be stuck paying a lawyer to clear your name. For example, once the thief has cleaned out your bank account they may resort to depositing empty envelopes into the bank machine in an attempt to steal more money. This can result in the bank placing a notice on your credit report regarding fraudulent use of the ABM. If you are not able to convince the bank that you are the victim rather than the perpetrator, this fraud notice on your credit report will create a huge problem that will haunt you for years.

Banks and credit card companies combatting fraud

Banks and credit card companies are working hard to try to protect themselves and their customers from fraud. They have computer programs that monitor buying habits and alert them if there is a significant change in buying patterns. Fortunately, over 90% of fraud is caught by the banks before the customer even knows what has happened.

One afternoon I received a call from American Express

asking me if I had my credit card with me. I pulled it out of my wallet and said yes. They said that they were cancelling my card number and sending me a new card with a new account number by courier that day. They said my card had been "compromised." Charges for hotels in Europe and the Carribean had gone through that afternoon. Their computer had caught the fraud. I thanked them for saving me a lot of headaches.

On another occasion, within a few seconds of finishing a call on my cell phone, the security manager of the cell phone service provider called me to ask me if I was in Mexico. I said, "No. I'm here in my office in Toronto." He said someone was making calls from Mexico to numbers in Asia. A computer program had caught the impossibility of making calls from two locations so far apart at the same time and had alerted the security people. The cell phone company cancelled my number and never billed me for the illegal calls from Mexico. Their computer had done its job.

Be vigilant

The 2005 Identity Fraud Survey Report - released by the Better Business Bureau and Javelin Strategy & Research found that, in spite of what most people think, most identity theft is conducted off-line rather than through the Internet, and that people who access their bank accounts online tend to detect the crime sooner thus minimizing losses. Having a low daily limit on ATM withdrawals and purchases (you can always call to increase it if you know that you will be making a larger purchase) and checking your balance daily on-line can limit your losses if someone gets a hold of your bank card.

While identity theft is one of the most upsetting and stressful things that can happen to you, and although you cannot protect yourself hundred percent, there are things you can do to reduce the chances of it happening. Be vigilant and keep an eye on your credit report.

The credit bureaus emergency contact info:

TransUnion
Fraud Victim Assistance Department
P.O. Box 338, LCD 1
Hamilton, Ontario
L8L 7W2
Phone: 1-800-663-9980

Residents of Quebec contact:
TransUnion Fraud Victim Assistance Department
1 Place Laval Ouest - Suite 370
Laval, Quebec
H7N 1A1
1-877-713-3393 or 514-335-0374

Equifax
Credit Information Services
Consumer Fraud Division
Box 190 Jean Talon Station
Montreal, Quebec
H1S 2Z2
Phone: 1-800-465-7166 or 514-493-2314

Student Loans

14

Most Canadians require some sort of help to pay for their post secondary education. Many people borrow money to go to school. They hope that by earning a degree they will be able to get a better job and make more money. These tuition debts are often referred to as "student loans."

According to a Canada Student Loans Centre survey, "Overall, an estimated 78% of CSLP (Canada Student Loans Program) borrowers reported that they would not have enrolled if they had not received a Canada Student Loan. Attendance at a private college appears to be especially dependent on the availability of a student loan with 87% of borrowers indicating that they would not have enrolled if they had not received a Canada Student Loan (as compared to 78% of public college students and 69% of university students)."

The Rising Cost of tuition

According to Statistics Canada's most recent data, tuition fees at Canada's ninety-two universities averaged about $14,000 per year. A four-year degree will cost over $50,000, not including the cost of books, accommodation, food, or transportation.

Investing in your education

Statistics Canada says that two out of three jobs now require a post-secondary education and that students invest in their education for several reasons, but the major ones remain getting the job they want and making more money.

According to the Society of Competitive Intelligence Professionals, a global non-profit organization, in 1997, the median income for a high school graduate in Canada was $49,500, $59,500 for someone with a Bachelor's degree, $65,000 for a Master's, and a Ph.D. earned $95,000.

Statistics Canada also says that tuition fees have increased by 115% since 1980. The latest Statistics Canada figures show that 1995 graduates owed between 130% and 140% more to student loan programs than 1982 graduates.

Two sets of rules

There are two sets of rules that apply to Canadian student loans depending on when the loan was taken out.

For student loans before August 1, 2000

Prior to August 1, 2000, student loans were administered by individual financial institutions (banks and credit unions). If your student loan was obtained prior to August 1, 2000, you repay the financial institution which administers your loan.

For student loans on or after August 1, 2000

The National Student Loans Service Centre (NSLSC)

looks after all Canada Student Loans issued on or after August 1, 2000. Your loan is administered by the Government of Canada through the National Student Loans Service Centre (NSLSC). Your loan will be repaid to the NSLSC.

Getting a student loan

The Canada Student Loan program says that to be considered for a Canada Student Loan, you must apply through your province or territory of permanent residence. Most provinces offer on-line applications. Applications can also be picked up at your post-secondary educational institution or your provincial or territorial student financial assistance office.

Credit screening

Under the current student loan program, as part of the application process, applicants 22 years of age or over, who have never been awarded financial assistance under the Canada Student Loans Program, will have their credit history assessed. Where a history of credit abuse is found, the applicant will be denied a Canada Student Loan.

According to the Canada Student Loan Program:

"Applicants will be denied a Canada Student Loan where their credit history shows at least three instances when an instalment on three or more debts (each of which is more than $1000) was more than 90 days overdue."

The screening is limited to the three-year period preceding application. When an applicant is denied financial assistance based on their poor credit history, the applicant is informed of the opportunity to have this decision reviewed. In the review process, if an applicant is able to demonstrate that their poor credit history is due to circumstances beyond his/her control, the applicant may then be eligible for financial assistance.

Your responsibility

You are responsible for notifying the National Student Loans Service Centre (NSLSC) when you change your address, your name, or your phone number, leave or transfer to another school or change your graduation date.

Student loans and bankruptcy

Student loans less than 7 years old are debts that cannot be discharged (erased) in a bankruptcy. These student loans must continue to be paid after the bankruptcy proceedings are wound up.

Payments

The Canada Student Loan Program says that:

"You must begin repayment of your student loans six months after you stop going to school-this includes graduating, leaving or taking a year off from your studies. Although you may intend to return to school next year, your first loan payment will still be required in the seventh month. When you return to full-time studies, your previous loans will return to interest-free status when you confirm your full-time enrolment."

Although there are no payments for you as a student until six months after you leave school, the payments will be due to start regardless of the reason why you are no longer a full time student. If you drop out and do not complete your degree, you are required to inform the Canada Student Loan Centre and arrange to start paying back the loan after the six months grace period.

Your obligation to pay in six months begins even if you do not have a job.

Interest

The government pays the interest on your student loan as long as you are enrolled. Once you leave school, there is a grace period of six months before you start to pay interest on your student loan.

Default rate

[handwritten note: 3m pastdue is in default]

At the end of the 2005-06 fiscal year Canadian students owed approximately $1.5 billion in student loans, of which 18% were in default. A loan is deemed in default when it is in arrears for three or more months. An incredible $297 million has been written off.

These numbers show that many students find themselves in the unfortunate predicament of completing their education and not being able to start making their student loan payments six months after graduation. They have every intention of paying, but just do not have the money. When the first of their payments is due, they simply duck and hope they do not get caught until they find a job. Just ignoring the notices that start coming is a mistake.

A collection agency will be assigned to collect from you. They are experts at finding you and your assets. In today's world of databases everywhere, not leaving a trail is very difficult. You can hide for a while, but eventually the collection agency will find you. It is far better to be up front with the collectors and negotiate some sort of payment arrangement rather than avoid them.

Help from the government

There is assistance available from the government if you have trouble making your payments because you have not found a job. This help is in the form of interest relief and a revision of terms to allow for temporarily reduced payments. These measures are intended to help students with loans in good standing. Also, your province or territory of permanent residence may offer additional assistance to help you repay any provincial/territorial student loans you may have. Contact your nearest National Student Loans Service Centre for a list of resources.

Prior to 2000 the bank collects its money

Student loans prior to August 1, 2000 are administered by the banks. When your student loan payments are more than ninety days in arrears, the bank requests the government to pay them. The bank collects its money from the government because the government guarantees these student loans.

The government wants its money back

Once the government has paid the bank, the government wants its money back from you. The balance of the loan is assigned to a collection agency for a commission fee.

The government's collection agency

When the government's collection agency receives your account to collect, they pounce on it because the collection agency gets paid a commission only if they collect. The first thing the collection agency does is notify the credit bureau that they have begun a collection action. This puts the collection action on your credit report.

After first attempting to locate your assets, the collection agency will demand full and immediate payment from you. I had a client who received a call from two collection agencies who demanded the exact amount my client had in her bank account. This was not a coincidence. The collection agencies had done their homework and knew exactly how much money was available.

The collection agency, acting for the government, can seize the money in your bank account, put liens on your house and car, get your tax refund and take and sell any other assets you have.

Your credit report and your credit score

After graduation, hopefully, you are working and enjoying a well-established credit record. However, if you have not looked after your student loan, sooner or later, a collection agency will contact you. The collection agency will notify the credit bureaus. This will have a serious negative effect on your credit report and your credit score.

Settling a student loan for less

Here is the process that has been successful in reducing the settlement amounts for clients who owed money on older past-due student loans. The government and collection agencies are often happy to collect at least a portion of the amounts owed and are often open to settlement offers. With these older student loans, often the provincial, federal and bank portions of the loan will be assigned to separate collection agencies. Each portion has to be negotiated separately.

Confirm the balance and the interest portion

The first step is to ask for documentation proving the exact amount you owe. Because there probably has been a lot of interest added over the years, it is important that you know exactly how much of the balance represents interest. This will help you negotiate with the collection agency.

Make an offer

Next, ask the collection agency if they will take payments. They will usually say yes. Once they have agreed that they will take payments, ask how much the collection agency would settle for if you paid them in full immediately. Explain that you do not have the money to pay them but you might be able to borrow it from someone (keep in mind that they will already know exactly how much money you have in your bank accounts). Most of the time, they would rather get a commission for sure right now than a slightly larger one later with a risk of not getting paid at all. Expect the collection agency to insist that this is a limited time offer, probably a matter of days.

Removing the collection action from your credit file

Get the collection agency to commit to removing any mention of the collection action from your credit report. Because the collection agency put the collection notice into your credit report, the collection agency can take it out. Obviously, you must get this agreement from them before you pay them.

Method and location of payment

Your negotiated agreement should outline the method and location of payment. This should include deadlines and who will pay the costs associated with the method of payment, such as bank fees.

Get it in writing before you pay

Before you pay the collection agency anything, get a confirmation in writing of the arrangement. The confirmation should have all the items you have negotiated, especially the removal of the collection notice from your credit report. Only then should you pay. After you have paid, get a written confirmation that they have received the payment.

Confirm that the collection notice is gone

Check your credit report afterward to make sure the collection agency took the collection notice off your credit report as promised. The written commitment from the collection agency that they will remove the collection notice from your credit report will go a long way to making sure everything you have negotiated gets done. After you have paid, you no longer have any leverage to negotiate anything.

If the collection agency does not remove the collection notice from your credit report after you have paid, present the collection agency with the written document. If you have to, get the owner or manager on the phone. Keep pushing. You want this item removed.

Remember, do not ignore the letters if you cannot make your student loan payments. The banks and government are usually quite willing to negotiate with you. All that the person in the collection department at the bank and the government really wants is to resolve your file and get it off their desk.

The Small Business Owner 15

There are different "rules" when you are self-employed. If you are self-employed, you are considered a higher credit risk than someone who is an employee.

One of my clients is a small business owner who employs seven people. He came to me for advice about getting a mortgage. The bank had refused to approve his mortgage application. While he and his employees all derived their income from the same business, most of his employees qualified for mortgages, but he did not.

I explained that the bank believes employees have a guaranteed weekly salary while the owner of the business does not. It is ironic to think that your employees, who depend on you for their pay cheque, may qualify for a loan that you as the owner of the business cannot get. You may find yourself having lower credit limits. You may be asked to pay a larger down payment and a higher rate of interest when you buy a home.

Creditors want stability

Although you may earn more, being self employed means that creditors fear that your personal income will vary from month to month. They want stability and predictability. They want to know that they will get paid in full, on time, all the time. As with all areas of credit the issue is perceived stability over time. Most new businesses fail within five years. Ironically, an employee who first gets a job will be considered stable after about a year, but a self-employed person will need a track record of steady revenue of at least two years.

Some of your income may not be considered

Because of the possible fluctuations in sales, part of your self employment income may not be counted toward qualifying for loans. So be prepared to work harder to convince a potential creditor that you are worth the risk.

Proving your income from self-employment

Obviously, proving what you earn is not simply a matter of your creditor calling your employer for verification. It includes providing a copy of your last two years notice of assessment from the Canada Revenue Agency (which means you will have been in business at least three years), as well as making available financial data such as bank account statements and personal audited financial statements.

As a self-employed business person you have more tax deductions than an employee, this often results in paying less in taxes, but it also means that your net income will be lower.

Although illegal, it is a common practice for some small business owners to "skim" some cash off the business by not ringing in some of the cash sales. This results in a lower net income. A lower net income means qualifying for less credit. It also creates a problem for you if you want to sell your business because the value of the business will be understated in your financial statements.

Total debt service

Another reason why you may not qualify for loans as easily as your employees is that your business debts may end up putting your total debt in relation to your income out of the acceptable range.

Getting credit

Start by being well documented. You will never convince a potential creditor that you can handle your finances if you cannot handle your business and personal financial documentation.

Be prepared to show how your budget will accommodate the loan payments and how you will make the payments in the event of a downturn in your business. If your spouse has a "job" rather than working with you in your business this can be a positive factor.

You may have to offer some collateral or security to establish your credibility.

Commercial (trade) credit

Wholesalers and manufacturers have developed credit management systems for commercial customers that are not applicable to consumers. Commercial customers (businesses) behave differently because they are often ongoing, repeat customers. For example, a consumer will buy flooring for their house perhaps only every five to ten years from a retailer. On the other hand, the floor covering retail store itself will buy stock several times a month. This kind of commercial credit is called trade credit.

The manufacturer or wholesaler's credit department

Credit cards have replaced the retail store's credit department. The retail store will not worry about setting a credit limit for the consumer who will use a credit card to pay. The credit card company pays the retailer and in turn collects the money from the consumer. The credit card company assumes all the risk.

Unlike the retailer, the manufacturer or wholesaler usually has a credit department which sets the terms of sale for its business customers. Payment from the business customer is usually expected within thirty days depending on the terms that are negotiated. These terms will reflect the manufacturer or wholesaler's need to control the level of risk associated with selling to businesses.

Commercial credit reports

Small business commercial credit reports contain information about the credit limits and payment records of the business. Except for the practical issue of cost, there is no legal restriction on the number of times a credit bureau member can request a commercial credit report for an individual business. Each inquiry will show up on the report. The individual owner's credit records are kept separate in a consumer credit file.

In addition to the credit bureaus, there are commercial credit reporting agencies such as Dun and Bradstreet who collect financial data on most small businesses in Canada.

Incorporation vs. Sole Proprietorship

Personal vs. business assets. If a business is a sole ownership, the assets of the owner are available to the lenders when they want to collect their money. However, if the business is a corporation, the personal assets of corporate shareholders (owners) cannot be seized by the corporation's creditors.

Personal vs. business credit reports. While a sole owner's credit report is important to a lender because it indicates how the owner pays his bills, the credit reports of the shareholders of a corporation will only be considered if the shareholders have signed personal guarantees (promised to pay personally if the company does not pay).

Which business form to use when starting out and when to incorporate depends on your personal financial situation. It will also depend on the financial performance of your business.

When first starting out, a sole ownership often makes

sense for a small business. Personal lines of credit can be used to establish lines of credit for the business. However, as the business expands and sales increase, incorporating becomes more attractive.

Two major advantages of incorporating are:

1) Because a corporation is a separate legal entity, the shareholders' personal assets are protected from creditors who are owed money by the corporation.

2) A single owner may have limited access to funds while shares of a corporation can be sold to provide capital to expand the business.

Two major disadvantages of incorporating are:

1) The costs of incorporating and maintaining records for a corporation are higher.

2) A corporation could pay a higher tax rate than an individual owner.

Establishing credit for a new corporation

As a new business, it may be more difficult for a corporation than a sole ownership to obtain trade credit from lenders. First, lenders can look for payment only out of the assets of the corporation. Second, the anticipated sales of the new business may not materialize as quickly as planned.

Personal guarantees

If your new small business is a corporation, you may encounter difficulties getting what you need at first without personally guaranteeing the corporation's debts. The bank and your lenders may ask you for personal guarantees if you have recently incorporated.

A lot depends on the assets that you first transfer into the corporation. If assets worth a lot of money are on the corporation's balance sheet, then the bank and your lenders will be more apt to give you a line of credit because the corporate assets are available to settle creditor claims for payment.

On the other hand, if most of the assets belong to you instead of your corporation, then your lenders will want personal guarantees from you to make those assets available to them for payment.

Personal guarantees break through the "corporate veil" of limited liability. In other words, the protection you enjoyed because you are a limited liability company is gone when you sign personal guarantees.

Supplier trade credit accounts

Your small business, whether it sells goods or services, can benefit greatly from supplier trade credit accounts. Retail stores buy inventory for resale. Businesses that sell services, such as an accounting firm, buy office supplies and computer equipment.

Not only are supplier trade credit accounts convenient, but they also provide a source of precious working capital. They let you save your cash to grow your business until the invoice is due. Theoretically, you will have time to sell the item (or provide the service) and pay with cash generated from that sale.

Your trade suppliers are usually happy to open an account for you. By making it easy to order with an open account and granting you time to pay, your trade suppliers hope to tie you in to buying from them.

Supplier trade credit account agreements

Setting up your supplier trade accounts wisely right from the start will save you money. Make sure that you understand the terms of the supplier agreement.

Negotiating the right agreement will go a long way to a better relationship with your suppliers and reduce the likelihood of negative items on your credit report.

Ten points to consider when negotiating your supplier trade agreements:

1) When will the invoice be due? Will you have the cash flow to be able to pay it when due?

2) Do you get a discount if you pay early? Is interest charged if you pay late?

3) What if there is an error on your invoice?

4) Can you return or exchange an item if it does not sell?

5) Is there a rebate or discount for buying in bulk?

6) What collateral is required?

7) Are you being asked for personal guarantees?

8) Are there other suppliers who can supply you with the same product or service?

9) How long a period does the agreement cover? Can you terminate the relationship early?

10) Is the agreement transferable to a new owner if you sell the business?

Payment terms

Your supplier trade agreement should always be in writing. It should spell out exactly when an invoice becomes due. Many supplier trade accounts are due thirty days from date of invoice. Some are due sixty days, some ninety days, or more, depending on the particular supplier. You should try to get as long a term as you can. The longer before you have to pay an invoice, the longer you can hang on to your money and make it work for you.

Date of receipt of invoice instead of date of invoice

If possible, get the supplier to agree to start counting from the day you receive the invoice instead of the date on the invoice because it can be several days before you actually receive it. You should strive to make that delay to your advantage.

For example, back in the 1990's when I worked in credit in the high tech industry, IBM had the following terms with its suppliers: "net thirty days from date of receipt of satisfactory invoice." This means that IBM would pay thirty days from the day it receives the invoice as long as the invoice does not contain any errors, such as the wrong price.

Of course, your small business will not have the same economic clout as a giant like IBM does, but it can't hurt to ask.

Define how an invoice is received

Make sure that the agreement stipulates what "receipt of invoice" really means. Does it mean the day an invoice arrives in the mail? Is an electronic invoice sent by email over the Internet acceptable? By mail is better for you because it takes longer. Electronic delivery is better for the manufacturer or wholesaler because not only is it instantaneous, but receipt can be "verified" by the computer.

Your strategy for paying your suppliers

Once you have negotiated the absolutely best possible terms for your business, your strategy should be to stick to those terms.

Many small business owners believe that paying their supplier invoices late helps their cash flow. It does temporarily, but there is a price to pay when it will come time to renegotiate the terms of your supplier trade account agreement. After looking at your payment record, your supplier may decide to increase the price of the product or service to cover the extra cost of financing. The longer your supplier has to wait for your payment, the less likely you will be to get a price break. In the long run, a small business will benefit from a good payment record through better pricing and probably better service. It is far better to negotiate the right terms up front.

Discounts

Discounts come in two basic varieties: "quick pay" discounts to encourage you to pay earlier and "volume rebates" to encourage your business to buy more. Both of these items should be spelled out in the supplier trade agreement.

"Quick pay" discounts

There are many variations on the discount percentages and due dates that you can negotiate for paying early. For example, the payment term "2/10;n/30" means that the face amount of the invoice is due in thirty days, but if payment is received by your supplier within ten days of the date of the invoice, the supplier has agreed to let your business take two percent off the face of the invoice.

Another example is "3/15, n/60", which means that the face value of the invoice is due in sixty days, but that you can deduct a three percent discount if your business pays within fifteen days.

Volume rebates

Volume rebates are "rewards" that a supplier will give you for buying in larger quantities or for reaching a certain milestone level of sales for the month or the year. The rebates usually are paid back to your business after the close of the month or the year when your purchase levels can be verified.

Your supplier trade agreement should say when you will be paid for your volume rebate and whether the rebate will be in cash or a credit to your account to be applied to future purchases.

However, in some instances, the supplier trade agreement may stipulate that your anticipated volume rebate will be taken off the face value of each invoice. This arrangement means that you are committing your business to a minimum dollar level of purchases for the month or year. However, if you do not reach that level of purchases for the period, the supplier trade agreement may specify that the volume rebate is then refundable and due back to the supplier.

Overdue interest

The conditions for interest to be charged on overdue accounts need to be spelled out on the supplier trade agreement. The Interest Act stipulates that your supplier cannot charge overdue interest unless it is agreed to in writing.

The rate of interest and how it is to be calculated (simple interest or compounded) should be negotiated. Too often, small business owners do not pay enough attention to this detail and end up paying too much interest when they are late.

Exclude disputed invoices from overdue interest

You should get your supplier to agree in writing that no interest will be due on disputed invoices. Disputed invoices are those that you are not paying until the supplier sends you a corrected invoice.

You should never have to pay interest on an invoice that contains errors such as a wrong quantity or price.

Exclude cost of collection and litigation

Your supplier trade agreement may ask you to agree to pay for any costs of collecting overdue accounts. You should not agree to this. Otherwise, your supplier will have no incentive to resolve issues with you and your business will be liable for all legal and collection costs.

Invoice errors

Invoices you receive from suppliers can have several types of errors on them:

- Wrong company name or location

- Wrong item shipped

- Wrong price

- Wrong quantity

If you feel that you do not owe an invoice, for whatever reason, it is important that you advise your supplier's accounts receivable department immediately. Otherwise, you risk that your account will be rated poorly by your supplier's credit department who will assume you do not have the money to pay and report a negative item on your credit report.

You should keep a record of the contact with the supplier requesting the corrected invoice.

Wrong company name or location

Your supplier's invoice may be billed to the wrong name. Your supplier may have sent you an invoice billed to an altogether different customer by mistake. For accounting purposes you need to receive a corrected invoice before you pay.

Wrong item shipped

If you receive something other than the item you ordered, you will need to return the item to your supplier at your supplier's expense. Your supplier should send you a credit note that confirms that your account has been credited for the returned goods. Your supplier trade agreement should spell out the return process and who pays for shipping.

Wrong price

If your invoice shows that you have been charged the wrong price, you have a couple of options.

First, you can refuse to pay until you receive a corrected invoice. The second option is to pay what you believe to be the correct price, which may leave a balance outstanding on your invoice. If the supplier takes too long to issue a credit to remove that balance, they could report the overdue balance as a negative item on your credit report.

I recommend waiting for a corrected invoice, although you can expect the supplier's accounts receivable department to put pressure on you to pay it. Not paying gives you more leverage to get the mistake resolved.

Wrong quantity

If your invoice shows that you have been charged the wrong quantity, again, you have a couple of options. First, you can refuse to pay until you receive a corrected invoice. The second option is to pay only for the quantity you received.

Right of return or exchange

If you receive merchandise from your supplier that is defective, or does not sell, you want to be able to return it for a credit to your account or exchange it for another item. Your supplier agreement should spell out in detail the conditions and the procedures you will need to follow to return or exchange merchandise.

Collateral for a small business loan

If you want a line of credit for your small business, the bank may want collateral. Providing collateral is giving the lender the right to take something of value that can be sold to pay the loan in case of default. For example, the bank may want to have you pledge your home. This means that, if you cannot make the loan payments, the bank can take your house and sell it to get its money back. Keep in mind, that if your business subsequently becomes a corporation, the bank keeps its right to the collateral as long as you owe money on the loan.

Competitive suppliers

The number of suppliers who can provide the same product or service to your business will have an impact on your ability to negotiate a better supplier trade agreement. If there are many suppliers vying for your business, it will be easier to get a better deal for your business. On the other hand, if there is only one supplier whose product is vital to your business, it will be more difficult to drive down the price or get better payment terms.

Life of your supplier trade agreement

The supplier trade agreement should stipulate the period during which the terms of the agreement are in effect. This will be necessary to adequately plan purchases and cash flow requirements for your business. Your marketing strategy will be based in part on your cost structure. You need to be able to count on that cost structure being in place.

The termination clause

You need to have a termination clause built into your supplier trade agreement so that you can exit the agreement without penalty. You may find another supplier of the same product willing to give you much better terms or prices. You have to retain the ability to end the agreement and do what is best for your business.

Transferability of your supplier trade agreement

Your supplier trade agreement needs to be transferable to a new owner if you decide to sell your business. For example, your supplier trade agreement may contain a provision for an advantageous price guarantee for the next year. This is a valuable asset that will make your business more attractive and more valuable to a prospective buyer.

Managing your accounts receivable

Get a credit application. If you grant credit terms to your customers, you will need to have them sign a credit application and agreement that gives you permission to obtain their personal credit report.

Make a credit decision

After assessing your potential customer's credit, you will have to decide if the amount of profit you are making on the sale outweighs the risk of not getting paid. This is not always an easy decision. Making the wrong credit approval decision can lead to spending more money on the collection process than the profit you made on the sale.

Sometimes it is better to walk away from a sale if there is any suspicion that you will not get paid. For example, if you earn a net profit of 5% on your sales, and you have $100 that you cannot collect, you have to sell $2000 without a loss just to recover that lost $100.

Make sure you get paid

After the credit sale has been approved, you will have to keep an eye on the account to make sure payments are being made as agreed. The collection effort can be time consuming and expensive. Keeping records and constantly reviewing the list of accounts is just the beginning.

Warning signs that you might not get paid include:

- Constant excuses
- Your calls not being returned
- Partial payments
- Unsigned cheques
- Broken promises

Try not to have too much of your accounts receivable concentrated in only a few customer accounts because you are more vulnerable if any one of them fails.

If your customers do not pay on time

Your cash will be tied up in your accounts receivable until the cash is collected from your customer. You may have to borrow from the bank to keep your business going until your customer pays.

The bank may want your accounts receivable as collateral to finance this type of loan. This means that the bank will take over and collect the cash directly from your customer if you default on the loan payment.

Factoring your accounts receivable

Another option is to sell your accounts receivable to "factors." Factors are companies that buy accounts receivable at a discount from businesses that cannot afford to wait for their customers to pay them. The amount of the discount can be very high, often surpassing the profit on the sales. Factors look for companies that are so desperate for cash that they are willing to give away their profit to obtain immediate relief from their creditors.

Long-term benefits of a good credit report

Building and keeping an excellent credit report will allow you to obtain the best possible terms. Your ability to sell at competitive prices and to preserve cash by using the financing offered by your trade suppliers will add value to your business.

"Wealth consists not in having great possessions but in having few wants."

Epicurus

16

Living Without Credit

A book on credit would not be complete without a discussion about living without credit. While credit is everywhere in our daily lives, if you are determined, it is possible to live comfortably without it.

I have a friend who grew up during the Great Depression. To this day he refuses to get a credit card. He has managed to buy and pay for his house. He has lived well and has purchased cars and has enjoyed vacations, none of which have been on credit. He has always saved up when he wanted to buy something. He does not have a bank debit card. He says that he does not trust today's computers. He is proof that you can successfully live without credit.

Paying for everything as you go has its advantages

- You never have to worry about who will be calling you about making your payments.

- You never pay "extra" for a product or service you purchase because there is no additional interest or fee when you pay cash.

- You can often bargain to get a "cash discount."

- There is no waiting for credit approval and no credit inquiry.

- You never have to worry about your creditor repossessing your home, car, or any other asset.

- You are free to sell any assets you have without worrying about getting permission from a creditor who might have a claim on the asset.

- You will not worry about where you will get the money for your next monthly payment.

No collection calls

Living without credit accounts means not being late with monthly payments. You will never get someone calling you at dinner time to ask when you will be making your overdue payment.

No finance charges

Because you will be paying the "cash price" for an item, you will not pay any interest or any additional fees. For example, a ten thousand dollar car can cost you over fifteen thousand dollars when you consider all the interest and fees that will charged to you over the life of the loan.

No fees

Lenders can also charge fees that are paid up front

or added to the loan amount. These fees are separated from the interest to give an apparent low interest rate. Many car dealers, for example, offer very small interest rate car loans if the fees are not taken into account. However, if the fees are taken into consideration, the overall cost of financing the vehicle purchase can be very high.

You can ask for cash discounts

Merchants are charged a fee by the bank on every purchase you make using the bank's credit card, ranging from one per cent to six per cent of the amount of the purchase. When you pay with cash, the merchants do not have to pay this fee. You can sometimes get a discount for paying cash by asking the merchants for a part of the fee they are saving on your cash purchase.

No credit approval required

Because you are not asking to buy on credit, you do not have to wait for credit approval. You are also eliminating the need for any lender to make credit inquiries on your credit report. Reducing the number of credit inquiries improves your credit score.

No possibility of repossession

Since none of your assets are pledged as collateral to guarantee any loans, if you lose your job, you never have to worry about a creditor seizing your home, your car, or any other assets. A drop in your income will not be as critical if you have no debts to worry about.

No monthly payments

Having no monthly payments relieves you of the pressure of coming up with those payments month after month. It also frees up cash flow that you can invest in savings. You can make long-range plans that will provide long-term financial freedom.

Strategies for living without credit

Delay gratification, avoid buying on impulse. Making the decision to delay making a purchase until you have saved up the cash is not easy. Sophisticated marketing departments know that the best way to coax consumers into making an impulse buying decision is to make buying their product or service fast and easy. Having credit available to use is a strong temptation for many consumers.

A mortgage-free home

House prices in the major cities are skyrocketing out of the reach of many average Canadians. Yet I recently met a man who owns a house in downtown Toronto. He has managed to pay it off completely within 10 years even though he has never earned much more than minimum wage. How did he do it? He made owning a home his first priority. He worked at two jobs for years to save up the down payment. He then rented out rooms to tenants. Now that the house is paid off he has cut back to one job, and enjoys the luxury of living without tenants. He has never owned a car.

Whether you are paying rent or making mortgage payments, housing costs are the single largest after-tax expenditure for most people. Canadians tend to want much larger houses than we actually need (compare our homes to those of the average European and you will see what I mean), which also results in larger heating and electrical costs and the tendency to accumulate more furniture and other possessions. Is it worth it? That is for you to decide.

While real estate is a good investment, renting is often cheaper than buying, especially since, as Canadians, we do not get the tax benefits of mortgage interest deductions that our American neighbours do. One strategy for reducing your housing costs while benefiting from real estate appreciation is to own a rental property which you rent out to tenants, but rent the house you actually live in from someone else. For example, you could buy a house and rent it to your brother and your brother buys a house and rents it to you. For both of you, your mortgage interest, maintenance and legal costs, and property taxes become expenses deductible from your rent revenue when calculating your taxable income. That way you both get the tax breaks.

Mortgage interest can triple the cost of your home

A $75,000 mortgage at a fixed rate of nine per cent over thirty years costs $217,244 to pay off, almost three times the original loan. Mortgages appear to be the only way to "own" your own home. However, "owning" is a relative term here. The bank has the greatest equity in the house over the longest part of the mortgage contract, not the person actually living in the home and making the payments.

You do not build up much equity in the early years. Equity is built up in the last years. The first ten years or so of payments on a mortgage go towards paying interest. It is almost as if you are "renting" the mortgage. Therefore, a good strategy to reduce the period of time to pay off your mortgage is to reduce the balance as quickly as possible. Your goal should be to reduce the portion of your mortgage payment that goes to interest and increase the portion that is applied to the principal. For example, if you get a bonus at work or you get an inheritance, use it to reduce your principal.

Bi-weekly payments pay your mortgage faster

Bi-weekly payments instead of monthly payments save you money. For example, let's assume that you have a $70,000 mortgage at 8.5% for 30 years, with monthly payments of $538.24. The interest over the life of the mortgage will be $123,765.48. If you make bi-weekly payments of $269.12 instead of monthly payments of $538.24, the interest will be $86,622.02. This will save you $37,143.46 over the life of the mortgage and your mortgage will be paid off in just over 24 years rather than 30 years.

If paying your mortgage off earlier is a good strategy, then not having a mortgage in the first place would be even better. One idea that was big during the back to the land movement of the 60's and 70's was to save up money to purchase cheap land in an area where the building code requirements were more lenient, move onto the land by using the simplest and cheapest temporary shelter available to you, and then build the permanent house on a pay-as-you-go basis. Unfortunately, there are a couple of major disadvantages to this plan. You will spend a larger proportion of your income on vehicles and transportation which are depreciating assets. Also, this method does not work if you live in a major metropolitan area, which is where most of the jobs are. Besides, as anyone knows who has actually tried it, it is very hard on your marriage trying to live in a construction zone for an extended period of time.

Cutting transportation costs

Owning a car is a huge expense. Could you live without a vehicle? The costs of owning and operating a vehicle include depreciation, financing, insurance, taxes and fees, fuel, maintenance and repairs. If you drive the national average of 24,000 Km a year, insurance companies estimate that a $21,500 car will cost you $6687.60 a year to drive or $33,438 over five years. Even factoring in alternate transportation costs such as public transit and occasional taxis, there are still many debts you could eliminate, or investments you could make, with the money you save. Alternatives such as walking and bicycling also have wonderful health benefits.

Buying a used vehicle

If you must drive a vehicle, you should consider purchasing a reliable used vehicle instead of a new one. Although a new car is easier to finance, a reliable used vehicle will reduce your transportation costs substantially, especially if you save up and pay cash for your used vehicle. A new car will drop thirty percent in value within thirty seconds of driving it off the lot. It will continue to depreciate at a very fast rate. When you finally pay off your car loan, the car may be worth very little on the open market or as a trade-in for another vehicle. Although the interest rate on used vehicles is higher, you will pay less interest overall because you will be borrowing less. Because car manufacturers want you to buy higher priced new cars, you can often get a new car with no money down. Given the higher loan amount, buying a new car can cost you far more in the long run.

Many people do not have the self-discipline to save up to buy a car, but they manage to make the car payments every month because they have to. Consider keeping your car an extra couple of years after the payments are finished and continuing to make the equivalent payments into your savings account which you can then use to buy your next car.

Leasing vs. Purchasing

Purchasing a vehicle means that you own the car outright after you have paid off the loan. When you lease a car, it is like a long-term rental. Your monthly payments allow you to drive the car during the term of the lease, but you must relinquish the car at the end of the lease.

If you lease, you will often be asked for the first and last payments as well as a "security" deposit. Whether you buy or lease, you will be responsible for insurance, fees, and maintenance.

Most leases offer you an option to buy the vehicle at the end of the lease. Unfortunately, the value of the vehicle may be less than the price you will be asked to pay. Often, a lease will stipulate the number of kilometres you are "allowed" to drive a year. If the number of kilometres at the end of the lease exceeds the total "allowable" kilometres, you will be charged a fee for every kilometre over the limit. This can be very expensive. You are also responsible for any damage to the vehicle such as scratches to the paint or marks on the upholstery. Many people choose to get these repairs done prior to handing in the vehicle because the charge for these damages can be substantial.

Sharing a vehicle

An alternative to owning and operating a vehicle is to "share" a vehicle when you really need one. If you are an occasional driver in a larger city, such as Toronto, Vancouver, or Montreal, companies have sprung up that allow you to "share" a car when you need it without incurring the fixed costs of ownership. Instead of paying for depreciation, financing, insurance, taxes and fees, fuel, maintenance and repairs, you pay only for the time you use the car and the miles you drive. How well this concept works out remains to be seen since these types of companies have only been around for a few years in Canada.

Only use credit for assets that appreciate in value

You should only use credit for assets that appreciate in value, never for items that depreciate. For example buying a home is a good use of credit. Its price will probably increase with time. Buying groceries or vacations on credit means that you will be paying long after the benefit has ended. Furniture, clothing, and entertainment are examples of items that should never be purchased on credit.

Budgeting

I remember reading an article about a woman who retired at age 32 with her house paid off even though she never earned more than minimum wage. She managed this through the strict use of budgeting. More strict frugality than most of us are prepared for, she even recycled her bath water to save money! But her example proves that it is not how much you earn that determines your financial future, rather it is how you choose to spend what you have.

Planning ahead how you will spend what you earn is the best way to control your monthly expenses. Having a monthly budget to allocate your hard-earned cash is essential to financial success. As well as providing you a sense of control, a budget allows you to reach your financial goals more quickly.

Conclusion - Achieving financial freedom

Keeping a credit card or two is not the problem; the challenge is having the discipline to use them judiciously. If you can discipline yourself to use credit wisely, you can break free from the burden of debt that most North Americans are saddled with.

Achieving financial freedom is up to you.

Appendix A - Sample Letters

Sample letter to a creditor.

Use this letter to ask a creditor to correct how your account is being reported to the credit bureaus and credit reporting agencies.

(Date)

(Address of creditor)

Attention: Credit Manager

Re: Account Number: _____

I recently obtained a copy of my credit report. I noticed that my account with you was reported as *(describe the way in which the account was reported on your credit report)*.

I have enclosed documentation showing that it should be reported as *(describe the way in which the account should be reported on your credit report)*.

If you agree that the information you have been reporting is inaccurate, please advise all the credit bureaus that you use so that a correction can be made on my credit report.

I look forward to hearing the results of your findings.

I can be reached at: *(List your mailing address and daytime telephone number.)*

Yours truly,

(Signature)

Sample letter to the credit bureaus

Use this letter to ask the credit bureaus to correct information on your credit report, such as the spelling of your name, your address, the name of your spouse, or the name of your employer, etc.

(Date)

(Address of the credit bureau whose report contains the error)

I am writing to ask you to correct an error on my credit report. I have enclosed a copy of my credit report on which the following item is incorrect:

(Incorrect item as it appears in your credit report)

It should be changed to:

(Item as it should appear on your credit report)

I have enclosed *(list the type of supporting documentation)*. If you need any more information, I can be reached at: *(List your mailing address and daytime telephone number.)*

Please send me a corrected copy of my credit report.

Yours truly,

(Signature)

Sample complaint letter regarding errors

For errors that you are unable to resolve, send this letter to the governing body that regulates Credit Reporting Agencies in your province. For best results, send a copy to the credit bureau(s) and the creditor in question.

(Date)

(Insert address for your Province)

I wish to file a complaint about *(name of creditor and/or credit bureau)* at *(address of creditor and/or credit bureau)*. My issue with this company is as follows:

(Clearly and concisely outline the issue you have been trying to resolve and how it has affected your ability to obtain credit, insurance, rent an apartment, get employment, or other setback. Make a sequential list of the steps you have taken and people you have contacted. Describe their responses in detail and supply their names if you have them.)

If you have received a number of complaints similar to mine about *(name of creditor and/or credit bureau)*, I hope you will help prevent this from happening to other consumers.

If you need any more information, I can be reached at: *(List your mailing address and daytime telephone number.)*

Yours truly,

(Signature)

Sample complaint letter regarding a collection agency

Use this letter to file a complaint with the governing body in your province that oversees collection agencies if you believe that a collector's behaviour has contravened the Collection Agencies Act. The addresses for each province are at the end of this appendix.

(Date)

(Address of provincial governing body)

I wish to file a complaint about *(name of collection agency)* at *(address of collection agency)*. My concern with this company is as follows:

(Clearly and concisely describe the behaviour of the collector which you believe has contravened the Collection Agency Act in your province. Make a sequential list of the events. Describe the event in detail and supply the individual's name if you have it.)

If you have received a number of complaints similar to mine about *(name of collection agency)*, I hope you will help prevent this from happening to other people.

If you need any more information, I can be reached at: *(List your mailing address and daytime telephone number.)*

Yours truly,

(Signature)

Addresses for Provincial Governing Bodies Regulating Collection Agencies and Credit Bureaus

British Columbia Business Practices and Consumer Protection Authority
PO Box 9244
Victoria BC V8W 9J2
Telephone: (604) 320-1667
www.bpcpa.ca

Alberta Government Services Consumer Services Branch
Manager of Investigations
North Field Services
3rd Floor, Commerce Place
10155 - 102 Street
Edmonton AB T5J 4L4
Telephone: (780) 422-9106
www.servicealberta.gov.ab.ca

Saskatchewan Registrar Consumer Protection Branch, Saskatchewan Justice
1919 Saskatchewan Drive,
5th Floor,
Regina, SK S4P 4H2
Telephone: (306) 787-5550
www.saskjustice.gov.sk.ca/cpb

Manitoba Consumers' Bureau
302-258 Portage Avenue
Winnipeg, Manitoba, R3C 0B6
Telephone: (204) 945-3800
www.gov.mb.ca/finance/cca/consumb

Ontario Consumer Protection Board
5775 Yonge St., Suite 1500
Toronto ON M7A 2E5
Telephone: (416) 326-8665
www.cbs.gov.on.ca/mgs

Quebec Office de la protection du consommateur
Capitale-Nationale - Chaudière-Appalaches
400, boul. Jean-Lesage bureau 450
Québec QC G1K 8W4
Telephone: 1 (888) 672-2556
www.opc.gouv.qc.ca

New-Brunswick Consumer Affairs
Department of Justice
P.O. Box 6000 Centennial Bldg
Fredericton, N.B. E3B 5H1
Telephone: (506) 453-2659
www.gnb.ca

Nova Scotia Consumer Complaints
Halifax Access Nova Scotia Centre
Reference: Consumer Complaints
West End Mall
Halifax, NS B3L 4P1
Telephone: 1(800) 670-4357
www.gov.ns.ca/snsmr/consumer

Prince Edward Island
Consumer Services Section
Office of the Attorney General
105 Rochford Street
P.O. Box 2000
Charlottetown, PE C1A 7N8
Telephone: (902) 368-4580
Web site: www.gov.pe.ca/infopei

Newfoundland and Labrador
Consumer Affairs
Trade Practices Division
Government Services Centre
5 Mews Place
PO Box 8700
St. John's NL A1B 4J6
Telephone: (709) 729-2600
Web site: www.gov.nl.ca

Yukon Dept of Community
Services
Box 2703
Whitehorse, YT Y1A 2C6 (C-5)
Telephone: (867) 667-5111
www.gov.yk.ca/depts/
community

Northwest Territories
Consumer Services Directorate
Municipal and Community
Affairs
P.O. Box 1320
Yellowknife NT X1A 2L9
Telephone: (867) 873-7118
www.maca.gov.nt.ca

Nunavut
Department of Community and
Government Services
Consumer Affairs
P.O. Box 440
Baker Lake, NU X0C 0A0
Telephone: (867) 793-3321
www.gov.nu.ca/Nunavut/English

Appendix B - Glossary of Credit Terms

Account condition
> Describes whether the account is outstanding such as open, paid, written off, settled, etc.

Account in good standing
> Account that is paid within terms.

AKA
> "Also Known As" (alias)

Annual fee
> Credit card fee charged once a year.

Annual percentage rate (APR)
> The rate of interest charged on an annual basis.

Authorized user
> Someone the credit cardholder authorizes to charge goods and services on the cardholder's account. The account is shown on the credit reports of the cardholder.

Balloon payments
> A single, lump-sum loan payment to be made at the end of a loan. Some mortgages are set up this way.

Bankruptcy and Insolvency Act
> Laws describing the way in which people who cannot repay their debts can get relief.

Capacity
> Refers to the ability to repay debt as it falls due.

Charge-off
>Action of removing the account receivable from "the books." These accounts are called "bad debts." It means the creditor has given up expecting to be paid.

Claim amount
>The amount a plaintiff is seeking or "claiming" from a defendant.

Collateral
>Something of marketable value (house, mortgage, furniture, car, piece of art, etc.) that you promise to the lender in case the debt is not paid as agreed.

Co-signer
>Sometimes called a co-maker, this person guarantees the debt of another. The co-signer will be asked to pay if the original lender does not do so. This item will show up on both people's credit reports.

Credit limit/Line of credit
>A credit limit/line of credit is the maximum amount a creditor will allow to be borrowed at any given time.

Creditworthiness
>The ability and willingness of an individual to pay their bills.

Delinquent
>Number of days past due based on the original credit agreement such as 30, 60, 90 and 120 days past due.

Discharge
>Court order erasing the debts after a bankruptcy.

Disclosure
>The obligation of a creditor and/or a credit-reporting agency to give you information about your credit.

Dispute
>A challenge to the validity of the information.

Equifax
>One of the two Canadian national credit-reporting agencies.

Finance charge
>Interest (usually included in the monthly payment).

High credit
>The highest amount that you have owed so far.

Instalment credit
>Credit to be repaid in payments.

Judgment
>A declaration by the court that the defendant owes the plaintiff.

Last reported
>On the credit report, the date the creditor last reported information about the account.

Lien
>A legal interest in property. Usually means that a security interest document is drawn up to provide a lender with collateral for a debt.

Personal information
>Information that is associated with you and can identify you, for example, your name, Social Insurance Number, birth date, etc.

Plaintiff
>Someone who issues a Statement of Claim against a defendant in court. In credit matters this usually refers to the person who is owed money and is going to court in an attempt to collect.

Public record items
>Tax liens, lawsuits, judgments, bankruptcies, and other registration of collateral or legal interest in property through the courts or with a government body. These are recorded automatically in your credit report.

Secured credit
>Loan with collateral.

Security
>Collateral that the creditor can get and sell to recover money if payment in full is not received.

Settlement
>Agreement to pay part of the original debt as a full and final payment.

Terms
>The original agreement between lender and debtor describing how and when the debt will be repaid.

Third-party collector
>Collection agency.

Trade line
>Line of information in a credit report describing the status of the debt such as balance, terms, etc.

Transaction fees
>Charges for using the lender's services (such as ATM).

TransUnion
>One of two Canadian national credit-reporting agencies.

Unsecured credit
>Debt or loan without collateral.

Index

A
action dismissed 29
adding positive information 72
address 62-63, 170
administrative fees 45, 102, 107
affiliated companies 21
age of majority 118-120
AKA 87
alias 87
annual percentage rate 101
application fee 102, 107
appraisal fee 108
appreciation 217
arrest 43, 143
ATM 161-163, 169
automated banking machine 161-163
automated credit decisions 14, 55, 87
automated credit scoring 55, 87
auto finance agreements 116, 144, 164
automobile sharing 217
available equity 117

B
bad debt write off 27, 141
balance due immediately 46
bank card 160
bank loans 91-93
bank overdraft protection 47, 49
bankrupt creditors 115
bankruptcy 28-30, 37, 71, 127-137, 182
Bankruptcy & Insolvency Act 130, 136
bankruptcy trustee 115, 130-132
bankrupt in process 131
behavioural theory 60
beneficiaries 124-125
birth certificate 165
bi-weekly mortgage payments 214
bondable 9, 36
bounced cheques 42-50, 102
business accounts 13, 151, 192, 195-205
business credit report 13, 151, 192-193

C
"calling" a demand loan 108
Canada Mortgage and Housing Corp 112
Canada Revenue Agency 8, 134, 190
Canada Student Loans Program 179-188
Canadian vs. U.S. credit reports 24
capital gains tax 113
car loans 116, 144, 164
cashier's cheque 48
change of address 62-63, 163
changing your name 87
child support payments 7-8, 21, 65, 134
civil litigation 164
CMHC 112
collateral 117-118, 204
collection agencies 1, 3, 21, 76-77, 140-141, 146-149
Collection Agencies Act, the 148-150
collection agency fees 141
collection agency harassment 146-149
collection calls 148
collection costs 45-46
comments on your credit file 65, 71
commercial credit reports 13, 192
commercial (trade) credit 13, 151, 192, 195-205
commission earnings 62
complain to the registrar 38-39, 150
compounded interest 213-214
computerized credit systems 14, 55-66, 85-87
Consolidation order 139
Consumer Affairs Ministry 39
consumer buying patterns 18
consumer credit 13, 16, 32-33
consumer proposal 136
consumer reporting agencies 36
consumer vs. commercial credit 13, 151, 192
contacting the Registrar 38-39, 150
conventional mortgages 110-113
corporate shareholders 193-194
co-signing 115

230

court orders 13, 21, 30-31, 37, 84, 133, 139-140, 142-143
CRA 8, 134, 190
credit bureau 11-25, 31-39, 55-56, 69-82, 85-91
credit bureau members 13-21, 70, 73
credit bureau membership agreement 18, 73
credit bureau revenue streams 18
credit cards 102-107, 159
credit check 11, 31-34, 72-73, 100, 159
credit consultants 76, 79, 83
credit counseling 128-129
credit files for marketing 18-19
credit inquiry 11, 31-34, 72-73, 100, 159
credit line closed by customer 26
credit monitoring services 170
credit rating agencies 53
credit ratings 25-31
credit risk class 57
credit repair firms 60, 67, 83-97
credit repair process 67-82
credit repair scams 60, 83-97
Credit Reporting Act, the 46, 36-39, 69
credit scores, marginal 14, 56
credit scores, threshold 14, 56
credit scoring 4, 12, 14, 22, 25, 55-66
credit scoring systems 14, 22, 25, 55-66
credit screening, student loans, 181
criminal offence 37, 42-44, 94-95
criminal record check 9

D

date of birth 90
death of a partner 123
debit card 160
debt discharged by bankruptcy 29, 133-135
debt service ratio 32, 64, 114, 118, 192
debt-to-asset ratio 32, 64, 114, 118, 192
debt to income ratio 32, 118
debt unpaid 29
default judgment 139-140, 142-143
deleting older items 70
demand loan 108
dependents 59, 124

depreciation 217
Depression, the 111, 209
discharge 29, 133-135
dishonoured cheques 42-50
disputed items 27-28, 70-72, 201
dispute after resolution 28
divorce 68, 121-123
documentation 72-75, 77, 80
driver's license 89, 164
due diligence 53-54, 91, 95

E

economic conditions 60, 63
effective rate of interest 101
electronic file 13
e-mail 167
employment credit checks 1, 9
employment, self earnings 62, 189-194
employment references, falsifying 94
employer, calling your 94, 148
employment, verification 94, 148
employment, self 189-194
Equifax 16, 18, 23-25, 55, 170, 178
Experian 24, 170

F

factoring accounts receivable 207
family support 7-8, 21, 65
Fannie Mae & Freddie Mac 54
Federal Trade Commission, US 157
FICO score 55-66
final bankruptcy hearing 134
first meeting of creditors 131
first mortgages 110, 113
fixing your credit report 67-82
Florida 43
foreclosure 54, 111
fraud 8-9, 20, 42-45, 51-54, 65, 83-97, 153-178
fraud warning 158-159
Freddie Mac & Fannie Mae 54
frivolous or irrelevant requests 79
full and final settlement 146
funds not cleared or funds held 42

G
garnishee 7, 139-140, 148
GE Mortgage Insurance Canada 112
government agencies 6-8, 36-39, 112, 134, 150, 179-188, 190
government security clearance 8
Great Depression 111, 209
gross debt ratio 32, 64, 114, 118, 191

H
harassment 146-151
high ratio mortgages 110-113
homeowner vs tenant 59
how long items stay on credit report 20

I
income tax 8, 94, 113, 134, 190
incorporating 13, 193-194
Identity Fraud Survey Report 177
identity theft 153-178
identity theft statement 172-174
information officer 150
information databases 22
inquiries 11, 31-34, 72-73, 100, 159
installment account 27, 102
Institute of Credit Management 155
insurance 6, 21, 125, 164
insurance, fraudulent claims 6, 164
insurance, life 125
interest 101, 201
Interest Act, the 101, 201
internet 13-14, 81, 167
investigative reports 21
invoice errors 197-203

J-K
joint bank account 122-124
judgments 7, 13, 16, 30-31, 37, 84, 139-140, 142-143
kiting cheques 44

L
Lacombe Law 139
laws governing credit repair firms 83

leasing vs. purchasing 216-217
legislation governing credit bureaus 36
licensing 8
liens 6-8, 12, 36, 118
line of credit 108
living beyond your means 9
loan application fees 107
Loan Brokers Act 107
loyalty cards 104

M
making payments 30
managing accounts receivable 205-207
marital status 59, 121-126
market value of property 114, 117
medical records 22
merchant fees 102-103
minor 118-120
mistakes on your credit file 12, 67, 81, 86
money back guarantee 84
mortgage 20, 109-115
mortgage backed securities 53
mortgage broker 34
mortgagee 110-111
mortgage insurance 112
mortgage interest 213-215
mortgagor 110-111

N
National Housing Act 111
National Student Loans Service Centre 181
negative items 67-68, 76-77
notice of assessment 190
not sufficient funds 42-50, 102
NSF cheques 42-50, 102

O
older items 70
ongoing credit checks 33, 100
overdraft protection 49-50

P-Q
paid in full as agreed 26
partnership 13

payments to a third party 116
pay stub, falsifying 94
perceived stability 61-62, 66, 190
permission 13, 32-34, 72-73
personal guarantees 195
Personal Information Protection and Electronic Data Act 149-150
personal info-reporting agencies 37
personal vs. business assets 13, 192-193
personal vs. business credit reports 13, 192-193
personal vs. business debt 13, 151
photo ID 91
PIPEDA 149-150
police 8, 20-21, 43-44, 67-68, 143, 155, 158, 163, 172
power of attorney 125
pre-approved credit 99-100
predicting delinquency 21
preferred creditors 132-133
privacy protection 76, 91, 149-150
professional licences 8
proposal for payment 136-137, 145
proposals in bankruptcy 136-137
property taxes 7, 36
public records 7, 12, 16, 28-29, 88
public utilities 6
quick pay discounts 199

R

"R1-R2- R3- I3" 26-27
"R9" or "I9" 27, 84, 137
real-time credit systems 86
receipts 72
refused credit 35
Registrar 38-39
remarriage 68, 122-123
removing negative info 67-68, 77
report card 11-12
repossession 36, 46, 64, 116-117
requesting an investigation 69
returned cheques 42-50, 102
revolving credit 26-27, 102

S

sales prospect lists 18-19
schedule 1 banks 41
schedule 2 banks 41
secondary identifiers 85
second mortgages 113
secured credit card 105-106
secured creditors 132
security clearance 8
security deposits 6
seizing assets 7, 139-140, 142, 148, 210
self-employment 62, 189-207
settlement agreement 145
signature loans 91-93, 108
simple interest 201
skip, out, tracing 20, 30, 62
Small Claims Court 84, 140, 142
Social Insurance Number 85-90
Social Services 8
sole ownership 13, 151, 193-194
stability 61-63, 66, 190
statement of claim 13
Statistics Canada 179-180
stop payment 49
student loans 134, 179-188
subpoenas 21, 139-140, 142
sub-prime mortgages 51
suing a lender 73
suing the credit bureau 74
summons 139-140, 142
supplier trade credit accounts 191-205
supporting documents 78, 173

T

tagging your credit file 158-159
tax department 8, 134, 190
tax evasion 8, 94-95
telephone 63, 121, 163
third bankruptcy 71
third party collector 141
thirty-day limit 69
too new to rate 26
total debt ratio 118, 191
trade credit 13, 191-205
transferring credit card balances 104

233

TransUnion 16, 18, 23-25, 55, 170, 178
trend information 18
trust companies 6
trustee's fees 131
two major credit bureaus in Canada 16, 23

U-V
unauthorized inquiries 72-73, 159
unique identifiers 85-86
unsecured creditors 132-133, 136
up front fees 107-108
U.S. credit reports 24
user fees 103
usury laws 101
using a representative 76, 79, 83
utility bills 6
vehicle ownership 164, 215-216
volume rebates 200

W
withdrawing permission 33
welfare agencies 8
wills 124
write off bad debts 27, 141
written permission 13, 32-34, 72-73

Credit for Canadians:
Everything you need to know to
fix your own credit report
and protect yourself from identity theft

Would your friends and family members benefit from reading this book?

We offer discounts when ordering multiple copies. For ordering information contact the publisher at **416-929-1202** or **www.nixon-carre.com**

Would you like to have Mike speak at your next meeting?

Mike Morley is an entertaining and informative speaker. He is available to speak to your service club, school, or other organization.

Mike can be reached at **416-275-1278**
or by email at **mike@mikemorley.com**

www.mikethecreditguy.com

www.mikemorley.com

Other books by Mike Morley:

Sarbanes-Oxley Simplified
ISBN 978-0-9737470-3-4   172 pages $29.95

Is it accurate? Are you sure? Can you prove it?
It isn't necessary to struggle through huge, painfully boring books filled with accounting jargon and legalese. This book describes, in plain language, what the U.S. Sarbanes-Oxley Act says, it explains why the Act came into effect, and shows what companies need to do to ensure that they are in compliance with the Act.

Financial Statement Analysis Simplified
ISBN 978-0-9737470-5-8   172 pages $29.95

Finally an accounting book for non-accountants.
This book translates the accounting language of financial statements into clear, easy-to-understand terms that anyone who needs to make well-informed financial decisions quickly will appreciate.

IFRS Simplified
ISBN 978-0-9783939-1-5   172 pages $29.95

Like it or not, **International Financial Reporting Standards (IFRS)** are coming and they will completely change how companies report their financial statements ... Are you ready?

If you need to get up to speed fast regarding IFRS then this is the book for you!

Published by Nixon-Carre Ltd., Toronto, ON, Canada
www.nixon-carre.com

CPSIA information can be obtained at www.ICGtesting.com
Printed in the USA
BVOW012049030213

312239BV00009B/112/P

9 780978 393908